MW01001270

Advance Praise for Encore Season

"Terri has written exactly the book I needed and at just the right time. My parents passed in their sixties, so I admit to facing this next chapter of my life with uncertainty and no small amount of dread, but Terri, in her candid, refreshing, relatable—and sometimes heart-tugging way—shows me there's nothing to fear. Opportunity and adventure awaits those of us with a bold spirit and an open heart. The best is yet to come."

—**Tracy Brogan**, *USA Today*, *Wall Street Journal*, and Amazon best-selling author

"A year ago I decided to "retire" from linear living (a.k.a., making a living) and began my years of 'rewirement.' Now in my mid-sixties I have been able to observe my parents and others as they age into their 70s, 80s, and like my Dad into their 90s and beyond. I'm celebrating the circular pattern of the seasons and distanced from the linear progression or steps of 'building a life' or 'success.' That's why I heartily endorse Terri's new book because we truly enter an 'Encore Season' if we make up our minds to do so. The best is yet to come. Armed with experience, wisdom and time, I'm seeing you can live life with purpose. Make a difference. Leave a mark. Seize the day. Within a different context (his comments were during a time of war), I think about the journey of my life and apply a favorite quote from Winston Churchill in November of 1942. 'Now this is not the end. It is not even the beginning of the end. But it is, perhaps, the end of the beginning.'"

—**Rick Vuyst,** author

"Whether we like it or not, change is inevitable as we age. Encore Season is an uplifting exploration of how to boldly embrace that change, discover new purpose and deepen relationships. Terri's willingness to share her struggles and strengths can help us all be more thoughtful as we "take a bow" and enter our 'Encore Season.'"

—**Cynthia Kay**, business owner, speaker, author of *Small Business for Big Thinkers and Stop Wishing. Stop Whining. Start Leading*

"Terri has interviewed me every Tuesday on the eightWest show for the past four years! We often discuss what an encore career looks like for my clients. Terri has used those insights to create this wonderful book to help YOU, not only enjoy every second of your next chapter but to thrive and win!"

—**Tom Jacobs,** president and CEO Jacobs Financial Services, retirement financial and insurance professional

"Terri DeBoer has done it again! This insightful book captures the brilliance, magic, and joy found in the final season of life, called the Encore Season. Terri's thoughtful metaphors, candid stories, and helpful advice will breathe new energy into those entering this long-awaited—dare I say, *the best*—season of their lives. May we all treasure our encores!"

—**Cortney Donelson,** owner and principal writer at vocem LLC, author of multiple books, including *The Billionaire's List*

"As a professional coach, and someone "old enough to retire," I have guided many people through the transition to 'retirement.' Frankly, I don't believe in the popular definition of *retirement*, and I don't think Terri does, either. I think you'll find *Encore Season* to be an inspiring guide that beautifully navigates the transition into this new phase of life. With its purpose-driven format, thought-provoking points, and personal stories, the book empowers readers to embrace their Encore Season with hope, adventure, and fulfillment. Whether it's pursuing new careers, hobbies, or relationships, this book will help you plan for great success and chase your dreams in this exciting chapter of life."

—**Tim Cosby,** president, Culture Impact, Inc.

"*Encore Season* is more than a guide—it's a testament to Terri De-Boer's inspirational journey. DeBoer, through her life story, calls us to embrace our later years as the thrilling encore of life. She navigates transitions with grace, inspiring readers to leverage newfound freedom to chase dreams and live their best lives. A must-read for anyone ready to take center stage in their own story, crafting an encore performance worthy of a standing ovation."

—**Shawn Sparks,** co-founder, Triad Partners

"Terri not only writes with grace and style, she's the living example of what she writes about. Growing up, growing out, and growing old (she's a long way from the latter) comes to all of us. *Encore Season* captures the importance of living through *all* the stages of life as if the best is always yet to come. The most important aspect of this is to never feel you've outlived your relevance."

—**Buck Matthews,** retired television and radio personality, author

"As someone who is in his Encore Season, I smiled many times throughout this book as Terri DeBoer leads the reader down the path of life here on earth, which all of us travel. Her successful career as one of the leading meteorologists and television personalities in her community is on display, and it is no surprise that she has become a successful author as she begins her journey through her Encore Season. Terri has been a wonderful role model for working moms but working dads (and granddads) will also benefit from *Encore Season!* This book will provide you with hope and a positive attitude that you too can have a successful Encore Season!"

—**Tim Selgo,** author of *Anchor Up: Competitive Greatness the Grand Valley Way*, inspirational speaker, consultant, formerly with GVSU Athletic Department

ENCORE
SEASON

Making the Rest of Your Life
...the Best of Your Life

Terri DeBoer

First paperback edition 2023

ISBN: 979-8-218-30571-0 (E-book)
ISBN: 979-8-218-30572-7 (Paperback)

Front cover design by Onur Askoy

www.onegraphica.com

www.terrideboer.com

Dedication

For my incredible family.

Watching each of you chase your dreams inspires me to perform my own encore.

"Twenty years from now you will be more disappointed by the things that you didn't do than by the ones you did do. So throw off the bowlines. Sail away from safe harbor.

Catch the trade winds in your sails. Explore. Dream. Discover."

—Mark Twain

Table of Contents

Acknowledgments

To my husband, Bill, for his love, support, and encouragement as I embark on my "Encore Season."

My children—Jacob, Jacqueline, Jennifer, Taylor, Ben, Jason—for filling my life with hope, joy, laughter, and love. Watching all of you dream big and work hard has inspired me to begin my Encore Season.

My grandchildren, for teaching me to slow down and enjoy the simple things in life . . . and for inspiring me to create a legacy.

My parents, Ronald and Helen Ferrucci, and my brother Ron, for a lifetime of unfailing love and support.

All of my colleagues from my decades in television broadcasting, for being such great teammates on my remarkable professional journey.

Tom Jacobs and the team at Jacobs Financial Services, for welcoming me into my "Career Encore": joining your efforts to help your clients financially prepare for their Encore Seasons!

Cortney Donelson, for sharing her incredible professional and creative talents to help shape my thoughts, ideas, and words into a meaningful manuscript.

Katie Cosgrove, for using her impressive literary expertise and skills to design a beautiful and easy-to-read book.

My greatest gratitude is for the peace and hope through all seasons of life that comes from a relationship with Jesus Christ and the love of our amazing Heavenly Father!

Introduction

In November 2021, I achieved a lifelong goal of becoming a published author when I released *Brighter Skies Ahead: Forecasting a Full Life When You Empty the Nest*. The inspiration for the book came from the emotional process I navigated when I became an empty nester. As I received feedback from readers and spoke to groups of people (mostly women) about the empty nest journey, it became clear that becoming an empty nester is not really its own season; instead, it's a time of *transition* into a completely different season.

The Encore Season.

Encore is a word that creates an instant mental image. It is a powerful and challenging word. If you think back to the concerts you attended, you might recall that musicians often save their "best song(s)" to perform *after* they have already finished the main part of the performance, after they've already walked off the stage. The stage lights go dark. The audience applauds and screams for more! *Then* the musicians walk back on stage and play their *best stuff*! Often, it's their most popular or most recognizable song.

As we make the transition into our fifties, sixties, seventies, and beyond, we are living in our Encore Season. This is a season that can be filled with hope and adventure. Just as the musicians come back on the stage to perform the best part of their concerts—after audience members think the show is over—many of us will get to live the best part of our lives in this season.

Most career experts (and governmental statisticians) agree that 10,000 people retire daily in the United States! Ten thousand people *every day*! That means millions of people every year are entering the Encore Season.

For some, the Encore Season begins by leaving a career we have worked in for several decades to enjoy a life of leisure or travel. Others will step away from the workforce to engage in meaningful volunteer or service opportunities. Still others will use the flexibility and freedom to study and train for employment in a new field—perhaps even starting a business of their own.

Often, the Encore Season will find us with more financial resources as most of us no longer support our children at this stage of life. And we can finally start tapping those retirement "nest eggs" that have taken up a portion of our budget for the past several decades!

The purpose of this book is to help you plan for great success in this new season.

The format is purpose-driven and provides thoughtful questions at the end of each chapter.

I hope this book compels you to look forward to the next season in life, using your newfound freedom and flexibility with time and resources to set new goals and chase new dreams.

SECTION 1: Encore Decision

A thriving new beginning can be and should be a time for amazing engagement, growth, connections, contributions, and amazing possibilities.

—**Lee M. Brower**

Chapter 1

Seasons of Life

sea·son (sē′zən)[1]
noun

1. one of the four natural divisions of the year, spring, summer, fall, and winter, in the North and South Temperate zones. Each season, beginning astronomically at an equinox or solstice is characterized by specific meteorological or climatic conditions.

2. a recurrent period characterized by certain occurrences, occupations, festivities, or crops: the holiday season; tomato season.

3. a suitable, natural, or convenient time: a season for merriment.

4. a period of time: gone for a season.

---

1. These definitions come from a combination of Google, dictionary.com, and Merriam-Webster.com. I used multiple sources to develop a full definition because the idea of seasons is so important for us to understand life's changes.

For everything, there is a season, and a time for every purpose under heaven: a time to be born, and a time to die; a time to plant, and a time to pluck up that which is planted; a time to kill, and a time to heal; a time to break down, and a time to build up; a time to weep, and a time to laugh; a time to mourn, and a time to dance; a time to cast away stones, and a time to gather stones together; a time to embrace, and a time to refrain from embracing; a time to seek, and a time to lose; a time to keep, and a time to cast away; a time to rend, and a time to sew; a time to keep silence, and a time to speak; a time to love, and a time to hate; a time for war, and a time for peace.

—Ecclesiastes 3:1–8

As a meteorologist, I've spent my adult life (the past few decades) obsessed with seasons. More than thirty years translates into 120-plus seasons. My professional life requires forecasting the always-changing weather in western Michigan, a part of the country that features all four seasons.

As a *television* meteorologist, I've spent that same amount of time navigating the tumultuous seasons of broadcasting and the media. When I started my broadcast television career, there were no cell phones, websites, social media, Netflix nor Google nor Amazon, and no Hulu! In today's media world, the explosion of technology has created so many sources for people to find information and entertainment; it's a challenge to keep viewers connected to local television.

Through all these changes, I've been fortunate to become an enduring constant in my local television market, even as the broadcast news industry has changed as dramatically and as frequently as the changing seasons and corresponding weather I've been forecasting. As with any successful career, I didn't do it alone. God has blessed me with supportive friends, inspirational mentors, and hard-working colleagues who have created an environment for stability and longevity. I will share stories from these relationships in the pages of this book.

As a working wife and mother (and now grandmother), my family has gone through the biggest series of changes over these decades—from walking down the aisle and saying "I do" to becoming a mother to three active children with demanding schedules, who I proudly say have now reached adulthood as incredible human beings. I spent at least twenty-five of the past years in the middle of a "whirlwind." As a professional family woman, I've experienced those decades through changing seasons.

Just as the weather and atmosphere are measured by seasons, so is life.

Life begins in a season we'll call "Growing Up." Like newly hatched robins in the springtime, in this season, we learn, mature, and prepare to launch into the world on our own as adults. Spring is a time of growth, development, and hope.

Just as late spring storms mark the weather of the season, the transition from this season into the next can produce the strongest storms. We might go through heartbreak as we search for a life companion or spouse. We choose a career path and work long hours as we start on the bottom rung of the ladder of success. Money is often in short supply; but as independent adults, we must provide for insurance, buy a car, pay rent, and start attacking those student loans. Professionally and personally, it can almost feel like we are drowning!

The next season could be called "Young Adult." It features the beginning of life as an adult—hopefully, one filled with ambition and dreams for the future. This is the summer of life. During this season, we launch our careers, often get married, and perhaps start a family. This part of life is a period of great transition, too, going from a "me-focused" perspective to an "others-focused" perspective, especially if we have spouses and children. Summer is often a time of much activity; the days are the longest, and it's a good thing because there is more to do than there seem to be hours in a day.

In nature, there is a sub-season that spans from summer into fall called hurricane season. This is when built-up atmospheric and oceanic energy is primed to unleash plenty of power.

The hurricane season of life is one best described as a complete "Juggling Act." This is when your children enter their Growing Up seasons. Like autumn, this season is filled with change. So much to do every day and, it seems for everyone, there are never enough hours in the day to get it all done. You can spend all day working, then the yard still needs raking. You can run from appointment to appointment, then still have to cook.

As a full-time working mother for many years, my life during the Juggling Act often seemed filled with utter chaos. I believe this is true for many people trying to keep it all together during these years when their kids are growing up. Sometimes, the thought of being all alone and having time to call your own, without other people relying on you, can seem like a far-off fantasy. But, like all things in life, the reality is the Juggling Act is just one season of life. It often lasts for decades, but it is temporary.

The transition from fall into the next season represents that time of harvest when we reap the benefits of our hard work and investment in so many different areas. This transition is another time of significant change. The clues we get from nature mirror what's going on in our lives. Days are getting shorter, and temperatures are getting cooler. The leaves on the trees are changing from the brilliant greens of summer to the colorful oranges, reds, and yellows of autumn. The tapestry is beautiful but creates melancholy as we grab for warm sweaters and jackets. This transition feels like an end is near. At work, we have achieved our career goals. At home, our children are graduating from high school and either continuing their education or starting a vocation—perhaps getting married and starting families of their own.

Winter days are short, dark, and cold. Sometimes we find it hard to believe there were ever birds, flowers, or green grass on the frozen and desolate landscape.

As we transition from late fall into winter, we are becoming empty nesters. We may be looking forward to a quick exit from a job we no longer find fulfilling, or we might feel uneasy about retiring from that career or job we loved. This is a time when some of us look back and reflect on all the seasons that have come before, wistfully wishing they might be granted a do-over for a season or two. Many remember their past with a mix of fondness and melancholy.

But before you kick back and settle into a long, nostalgic look back, know this: There is an exciting season on the horizon. It's just now getting underway. It's called the "Encore Season!"

Re-Entering the Spotlight on the Stage

If we are not careful, as we enter the Encore Season, we can squander these years in life since we don't have as many benchmarks or looming milestones to mark our progress. There can be the temptation to live waiting for the next storm to hit or the next big adventure to happen. From one day to the next, we may have some changes and challenges that demand our attention or disrupt the flow, but mostly, one day will flow into the next and the next, like living through the daily changes in the weather, or even the seasons. For example, as we move through summer, we may not notice the sun setting a minute or two earlier each day. But, by late fall, there's no mistaking the fact it's dark well before we sit down for dinner, dark even before the time our golf league teed off in the summer!

To take advantage of these years of our lives, we need to create new goals and permit ourselves to chase new dreams. This is a great time to search our souls to rediscover or redefine our passions. We might try something new or circle back to something we had put on hold for a few decades.

Most of us have heard the phrase "bucket list" before. It's the list people craft of all the things they want to do before they "kick the bucket." This list often includes important goals, like skydiving or traveling through Europe or visiting Hawaii. While those big items are great aspirations, smaller activities that can be incorporated into a daily or weekly routine will provide a boost to our quality of life too! Think about picking up the guitar again, working on your pickleball game, taking a class at the local community college (or even finishing that degree you've always wanted to earn), becoming a volunteer for an organization that could use your passion and expertise, joining a bowling league, or even starting a business.

PLANNING YOUR ENCORE

- Open an old photo album and find yourself in pictures from when you were in elementary school or high school. Try to remember what *you* wanted to do or be "when you grew up."

- Take out a notebook and write a list of the things in life you would like to achieve in the Encore Season.

- Write a step-by-step set of actions you need to take to accomplish the things on your list. If you don't know every step you need to take for a certain goal, try to write the first few steps you need to take to reach your goal.

Many people will never learn the lessons meant for them in this lifetime, nor become the person they were meant to be, simply because they are too busy being someone else.

—Suzy Kassem

Chapter 2

What's Happening Now and What's Happening Next

What's happening now is what happened before, and often what's going to happen again sometime or other.
—**Orson Welles**

When we are in the Young Adult season, we are in the beginning stages of our journey into adulthood. We may take college classes, start a job, or even embark on the start of our careers during this period in our lives.

For many of us, this is a time of self-discovery and self-improvement. It is also the time when we are self-centered, self-absorbed, and hopefully self-reliant. The *why* of this time is because this is our *alone season*, also known as the "Sub-Season of Self" or the "Sub-Season of Me." The life we have before us is, for the most part, an empty canvas.

We have the opportunity to try new things. If we decide we are on the wrong path or want to change the direction we are heading, we can often do so with minimal impact on anyone else.

This was why my life journey through my early twenties was relatively easy to navigate. I was bored with accounting, so I dropped out of college. While on that educational hiatus, I jumped from job to job, making connections with people who would ultimately point me in a new direction. After finally graduating with a degree in television news broadcasting and working for a couple of years, I pursued a specialized course of study in meteorology. When I made that decision, I devoted extra time, energy, and money to get advanced knowledge and training. I didn't have to support anyone else, nor did I have to get approval from anyone to follow this new dream. Since I was working in a television market much bigger than an entry-level market, I expected to have to move to a much smaller city to transition from a news reporter to an on-camera meteorologist. Since I was independent and unattached, I was not the least bit worried about taking that next step in my career upon the completion of my certification in Broadcast Meteorology.

Of course, I did not know I would fall in love with and marry a single dad just a few months into my program. I should say I fell in love with the total package of this sweet little boy and his dad. Because our love story included a child, we decided to get married fairly quickly. So less than one year after meeting these two special people, we became an official family!

Suddenly, the answer to the question of "What's coming next?" had dramatically changed for me. I was no longer in the Sub-Season of Me. I had made the transition into the "Sub-Season of We." My status as alone and independent had changed; I was married with a child.

Biology worked quickly for us, and less than two months after our wedding day, I was expecting a baby. I was now a full-time working wife and mother, devoting my spare time to a course of study that seemed like a waste of time, energy, and money. Finishing my meteorology training no longer came with the guaranteed opportunity of making the change from news to weather on air. Still, my husband and I decided I should follow through and complete the program.

PERSISTENCE

While earning my certification in Broadcast Meteorology, I learned an essential term for forecasting the weather: *persistence.* If you predict that today's weather will be repeated tomorrow, you will be correct a majority of the time. This is considered one of the most accurate techniques for short-term weather forecasting in the business. So when a meteorologist embraces the term *persistence*, they are indicating the current weather conditions are likely to continue. That the four seasons during any given year often feature a high number of stretches of sunny and dry days or cloudy and cool days point to the reliability of the persistence model of forecasting.

When we apply persistence to our lives, we are committing to a course or action, despite difficulty or adversity. As a new wife and mother, persistence for me often meant the daily cycle of work, studying, cooking, cleaning, shopping, playing, and nurturing my new family.

Perhaps you look back on those days in your life and, like me, draw a comparison to the famous Bill Murray movie, *Groundhog Day*, in which life became a series of the same day, repeated over and over.

THE ONLY CONSTANT IS CHANGE

Of course, we know even the most persistent weather pattern (or series of life circumstances) eventually breaks down. Just like the weather changes, so too does life. Preparing for and forecasting changes in life involves a similar set of steps as forecasting the weather.

Before digging into the atmospheric conditions for specific time frames in the future, the most essential starting point is the current situation. Not only is it important to look outside at *what is happening*, but it's also imperative to figure out *why* the weather is behaving the way it is. For example, if it's raining, what is causing the rain? Is it an approaching warm front or a lake-breeze convergence? Is it a pop-up instability shower or the beginning of a more intense line of storms?

In weather forecasting, understanding the *why* of the *now* is an integral part of correctly figuring out the *what* of the *next!*

Understanding the *why* of the *now* is an integral part of correctly figuring out the *what* of the *next*.

Meteorologists describe the atmosphere as a system in motion. That means there is always a "What's coming next?" to track. As we consider the journey of our lives, perhaps most importantly as we enter the Encore Season, those are the two questions we need to always be asking ourselves:

- What's happening now?

- What's coming next?

In my own life, I have spent the majority of the past three decades delivering West Michigan's "wake-up weather" on the market's number-one morning newscast.

Professionally, while there has been significant *persistence* in my career at WOOD-TV, my family expanded to include another daughter, two more sons, and two grandsons. My children grew up, finished college, got married, and began their adult lives as I entered the Empty Nest season.

In this season, one of the most common questions people ask me now is "When are you going to retire?" These days, I think about my Encore Season frequently, especially as I am stepping away from my decades-long career in television news and starting in an entirely different industry.

PLANNING YOUR ENCORE

- Describe your philosophy regarding change. Are you a creature of habit? Do you like things to happen the same way, every time? How do you react when change happens *to* you, especially in an area where you are happy with the "status quo?"

- Which areas of your life challenge you to have persistence?

- Think about "What's happening now"; try to imagine "What's happening next."

All changes, even the most longed for, have their melancholy, for what we leave behind us is a part of ourselves; we must die to one life before we can enter into another.

—Anatole France

Chapter 3

Evaluating Your Natural Resources

Retirement is wonderful if you have two essentials: much to live on and much to live for.
—Author Unknown

Is the Encore Season a time when you are celebrating *abundance*?

For many of us, the Encore Season might be the first time in our adult lives when we discover we have "left-over resources." Similar to food packaged up after a nice meal to be enjoyed later, we discover we have extra helpings of those things that were in scarce supply during the Young Adult and Juggling Act seasons!

It's almost one of life's greatest ironies in the later years of life, especially for parents; when our children were growing up, we were short on time, money, and energy. For many of us, the Juggling Act season was when we stretched all of our budgets to meet the multitude of our significant obligations, from financial budgets to allocated hours in a day. As we advanced in our careers, we often made more money and perhaps worked fewer hours.

In the Encore Season, are those once-scarce resources now available in more abundance? Or are our obligations so much less that our resources just don't seem to be as stretched?

TREASURES

Entering the Encore Season will mean tapping that "nest egg" you saved through your working years. Many of us set aside a portion of our earnings "paycheck after paycheck," sometimes for decades, to build up accounts from which to enjoy our "Golden Years." Now that those working years are over (or nearly over), there are important decisions you will need to make about your investments!

PROTECTION

You have worked hard and sacrificed a portion of your earnings to build up the savings you plan to spend in retirement. If your accounts are still invested in the stock market, this is the time in life to consider moving at least some of them to a much more protected place—a place where there's virtually no chance of losing any of what you have accumulated in those investment accounts during the turbulence that can be the stock market. Tom Jacobs is a dedicated retirement financial and insurance professional I know in West Michigan who believes that, for most people, Fixed Indexed Annuities[1] can serve as a protected place for retirement dollars. These vehicles are backed by

---

1. Tom Jacobs. Retirement Domination: Play to Win with Your Retirement, Tom Jacobs 2020.

the financial strength and claims-paying ability of the issuing company, which guarantees your money won't lose its value because of a declining stock market. Not only that, but an annuity also offers the opportunity to receive a continual stream of income for the rest of your life. Obviously, there's more to know about how these work, including their costs and limitations, but they're worth looking into as you approach retirement and need to protect your hard-earned retirement savings.

SPENDING

Instead of holding a tight grip on those retirement savings, come up with a list of how you would like to spend your money! Do you want to travel the world? Buy a second home somewhere warmer? Or colder? Get that sports car you have always wanted? Start college funds for your grandchildren?

There's no such thing as spare time, no such thing as free time, no such thing as downtime. All you got is a lifetime. GO!
—**Harry Rollins**

TIME

As we settle into our Encore Season, there comes the realization that our time on this planet is growing shorter. That we have gotten to this point of transitioning into a "next season" is a blessing in itself. If we are not careful, it can be easy to squander these precious days without accomplishing many meaningful goals.

"The days are long; the years are short" used to be a phrase I often quoted when my children were young. It referred to the chaotic daily demands of being a full-time working mother of three very active children in the Juggling Act. It was a "life on the go," filled with adrenaline and short on downtime. There was too much to do and not enough hours in the day.

When my children moved away to college, there was a complete flip of the script. Suddenly, there were too many hours in the day and not enough to do. Still working full time, I found fulfillment in my job as a television meteorologist and pursued my literary career, becoming a published author of multiple books. Eventually, I also filled my downtime with more social and leisure activities.

PLANNING YOUR ENCORE

- What does your financial picture look like for the Encore Season? Do you remember how challenging it was to stretch the dollars during the Juggling Act season?

- Come up with a "Bucket List" of ten items you would like to experience or accomplish.

- Create a "budget" of the financial and time cost for each of those items. Then create a timeline for doing each one!

Don't tell me where your priorities are. Show me where you spend your money, and I'll tell you where they are.
—James W. Frick

Chapter 4

The Encore and the U Curve

The curve seems to be imprinted on us as a way to repurpose us for a changing role in society as we age, a role that is less about ambition and competition, and more about connection and compassion.

—**Jonathan Rauch,** *The Happiness Curve: Why Life Gets Better After 50*

The emotional challenges we feel as we enter the Encore Season may also correspond with natural emotional cycles tied to reaching this chronological time in our life. We've all heard of the midlife crisis. We see the evidence and hear the jokes about some men reaching a certain age (about fifty) and trying to recapture the glory days of their youth by getting a gorgeous young girlfriend or perhaps a shiny new sports car. For women, it can be getting a facelift or Botox to combat the anxiety caused by the signs of aging, like wrinkles. To top it all off, this time in our lives is happening when we are emptying the nest and, for women, going through menopause, thus creating the perfect storm for emotional distress.

Most of us are familiar with menopause, but research regarding "The Happiness Curve" is not as widely familiar. While menopause impacts women (and indirectly their partners), the Happiness Curve impacts men *and* women. Let's begin there.

THE HAPPINESS CURVE

Research reveals a U-shaped curve when plotted with our feelings of life satisfaction as we go through each decade of life. The front part of the curve begins at a high point, when we are in our teens and early twenties, the Growing Up season. Then there is a steady downturn with each passing decade where life satisfaction drops. That downward trend coincides with the Young Adult and Juggling Act seasons, our late twenties, thirties, and forties. The bottom of that curve corresponds with turning fifty, just as many of us are likely still firmly entrenched in our vocations but maybe counting down to the Encore Season.

UPWARD TREND

Then something amazing happens! As our fifties continue, the line graph trends upward in satisfaction. As the year-by-year data is plotted, there is a corresponding increase in happiness, satisfaction, and joy in life. This upward trend continues into our late fifties, sixties, and even seventies. The data suggests we are as happy in our sixties and seventies as we were in our teens and twenties. This data comes from research conducted worldwide, across many societies, and spanning all socioeconomic levels. Research even shows chimpanzees and orangutans have the same shape in their happiness curves. (However,

I'm not sure how researchers determined when gorillas have a midlife mal
aise!)

HAPPINESS RESEARCH

One book that documents this research is *The Happiness Curve*.
Researcher Jonathan Rauch analyzed data and made these claims,
pairing different emotions and satisfaction levels with different life
stages[1]. In his book, Rauch reports the downturn in our late twenties
and thirties seems to be when we start our careers and families, or as
we struggle with the financial burdens of paying a first mortgage and
car payments and saving for college. At this time in our lives, Rauch
points out that as we struggle to get our careers off the ground, we
are sleep-deprived and on stress overload. As we head through the
downturn continuation, the bottom-most point in this curve occurs
for most of us just as we are emptying the nest. By the time we reach
this point in the curve, this downward spiral of satisfaction has been
decades long. We may believe those feelings of discontentment, sadness, depression, and anxiety are our new normal. It's hard to imagine
happiness and joy again. It's almost ironic to consider the research
from Rauch points to the Juggling Act years as the most difficult for
most adults; yet we look backward during the beginning stages of the
Empty Nest transition and remember them as the "good old days."
The most promising part of Rauch's research proves this transition
from the Empty Nest to the Encore Season is the beginning of our
turning the corner toward a happier life.

---

1. Rauch, Jonathan. The Happiness Curve, Thomas Dunne
   Books, May 2018

LOOKING FORWARD TO THE REBOUND

So why does this happen to us? A big part of it is that we stop so many of the activities that create stress, and we aim for a simpler life. This might be because an empty nest means we have fewer people to care for every day, so we feel less responsibility. Or it might be because, by this point in our lives, we are established in our careers and no longer feel the anxiety about performing or over performing.

Of course, the emptiness of the home goes along with fewer people depending on us, but the flip side of this feeling of solitude can be liberating. One other aspect of the transition into the Empty Nest and eventually the Encore Season is that we have new relationships that renew our sense of purpose. This is the time many of us may have grandchildren, bringing the return to the energetic activities that bring joy in these new lives and relationships.

MIDLIFE AND MENOPAUSE

Experts in women's health point to the Encore Season as coinciding with the significant physical and emotional phases of menopause. Dr. Renee Elderkin, MD is an attending physician and faculty member at the University of Michigan-Metro Campus and an associate professor at Michigan State University. She cares for women through every stage of life, from puberty to childbearing years and finally into menopause. Dr. Elderkin says one of the most important relationships as we age is one with a physician with whom we can honestly discuss *all* aspects of life. As an active member of the Board of Obstetrics/Gynecology and the American College of Obstetrics/Gynecology, Dr. Elderkin understands each season comes with feelings of grief, unworthiness, and uncertainty about the future.

For women entering the Encore Season in life, the biology of menopause produces dramatic physiological changes that, in turn, produce significant mood fluctuations. In her book, *I Want to Age Like That! Healthy Aging through Midlife and Menopause*[2], Dr. Diana Bitner, owner of True Women's Health[3], provides a thoughtful guide through the challenges of the physical transition into midlife. Dr. Bitner, a certified menopause practitioner for the North American Menopause Society, has developed specific treatment programs for women going through menopause. As Dr. Bitner discusses, most women will face challenges around their waistline and in the bedroom as they go through this transitional period in life, including mood changes, hot flashes, decreased sex drive, and night sweats. As with the other aspects of moving from the Juggling Act season through the Empty Nest transition and into the Encore Season, Dr. Bitner and Dr. Elderkin point to this stage as a normal and temporary transition, which most women can navigate with the right information, counsel, mindset, and support. If you are struggling, there is help available. You don't need to suffer or make a go of it alone.

HOPE FOR THE FUTURE

For people going through the transition into the Encore Season and still feeling on the downward emotional spiral, hang in there! Research

2. Bitner, Diana. 2020. I Want to Age Like That! Healthy Aging through Midlife and Menopause. Apple Valley, California: Splattered Ink Press.

3. "Complete Healthcare for Women by Women." True Women's Health. https://truewomenshealth.com/.

shows the upward march on the happiness curve is just around the corner.

PLANNING YOUR ENCORE

- If you think of your emotions in terms of a plotted line, how would you describe the direction that line is heading?

- Can you feel the natural cycles of aging? If you are a woman, how did (is) menopause impact(ing) your life? Do you feel out of sorts and unbalanced at times, not able to point out an explanation?

- Take out a notebook and start writing out what you're feeling and experiencing; try to name the motions and describe the physical changes.

You're also going to come to find yourself with the freedom to care about what matters most to you and pursue those goals, and not pursue the goals that other people say should matter to you.
—**Jonathan Rauch,** *The Happiness Curve: Why Life Gets Better After 50*

SECTION 2:
Encore Purpose

If you can't figure out your purpose, figure out your passion. For your passion will lead you right into your purpose.

—**Bishop T. D. Jakes**

Chapter 5

Discovering an Encore Purpose

The Bible says that as long as your heart is beating, God has a plan and purpose for your life ... to grow personally, to get to know God, to serve others, and (to) make the world a better place.

—Pastor Rick Warren

What on earth am I here for? This question is likely one we wrestle to answer as we enter the Encore Season. After decades devoting ourselves to our jobs or careers, raising children, and keeping a household running, figuring out a new purpose in life is essential, albeit often difficult.

Pastor Rick Warren is the author of the *New York Times* best-seller, *The Purpose-Driven Life*. This book is a forty-day spiritual journey to help transform the reader's answer to one of life's central questions: "What on earth am I here for?"[1]

---

1. Warren, Rick. 2000. The Purpose-Driven Life. Grand Rapids, Michigan: Zondervan.

Pastor Warren believes the most successful purposes will be aspirational and inspirational, combining our talents, passions, and skills to find something we love to do *and* are skilled at doing. The goal of the book and the process is to help readers figure out how to fit the pieces of life together to find meaningful ways to impact others' lives.

OUR PURPOSE AS A PARENT HAS CHANGED

During the years we raise our families, it is easy to see we may have multiple purposes, with most primarily designed to meet the creature needs of our children:

- Food

- Shelter

- Safety

- Education

- Transportation

- Extracurricular activities, like sports, music, theatre, dance, and other arts

- Emotional support and comfort

- Guidance and wisdom

- Structure and discipline

When your children are growing up, you have the social role of being the most essential person in another human's life. Of course, when our children are infants, they rely on us for everything. That's the case even through the toddler years. During this period, most children become a little more self-sufficient. They feed themselves, even though we still need to purchase, prepare, and provide the food; they learn how to go to the bathroom by themselves, and they walk, talk, and play. Talking brings a new level of engagement because they can carry on conversations with us.

Eventually, they go off to school, and year by year, our kids need us a little less. During those years they move toward independence, our primary mission will change, but our kids still give us a primary sense of purpose. Exhausted and overwhelmed with all the tasks we need to do, most days are packed with more to do than time to get it all done. The demands during this stage in life give us purpose.

As our children become independent adults and move away to start their young adult seasons, we find other activities to fuel our need to be needed. For those of us who have found identity and meaning in our jobs or careers, deciding to step away from that career and into retirement can bring another painful time of transition.

One trap many of us fall into during the Encore Season is believing we don't have a purpose.

PRAY FOR A NEW PURPOSE

Have you considered that at this point in your life, someone else may need what you offer? A call to any church's office will help you find opportunities to help others in your community—people who would find help offered by someone who is caring and experienced to be a gift from God.

As Warren says in his book, "God wants to use you to make a difference in his world. He wants to work through you. What matters is not the duration of your life, but the donation of it."

Opportunities to be used by God and to find a new purpose may include:

- Committing to a few hours of childcare for the overwhelmed single mom.

- Taking a meal and chatting with a senior neighbor or at a shut-in.

- Mentoring a child in school through a program like Kids Hope.

- Grocery shopping for a young family or house-bound senior.

- Visiting people in the hospital.

- Making and serving meals following a memorial or funeral service.

- Writing letters to a prisoner.

- Taking in a foreign exchange student.

- Becoming a foster parent.

INVEST 40 DAYS IN DISCOVERING YOUR PURPOSE

On Day One, Warren begins by offering a reassuring reminder that we are on this planet because of an almighty Creator, God. For those of us entering our Encore Season, wondering what's left in life now that our time of raising our children and full-time work is over, Warren states a biblically based piece of truth. "It's not about you. The purpose of your life is greater than your personal fulfillment, your peace of mind, or even your happiness. It's far greater than your family, your career, or even your wildest dreams and ambitions. If you want to know why you were placed on this planet, you must begin with God. You were born by His purpose and for His purpose."[2]

At the church Rick Warren founded, Saddleback, there is a special program designed for members who are newly retired as well as for those who are already settled into the Encore Season. It's called the **P.E.A.C.E**. Program:[3]

- **P**lant churches that promote reconciliation.

- **E**quip leaders.

- **A**ssist the poor.

- **C**are for the sick.

- **E**ducate the next generation.

As I am entering the Encore Season, I find my greatest desires are to find:

- A purpose that will fulfill me and help others.

- Deeper relationships.

- Peace.

---

2. Laura, Robert. "Pastor Rick Warren Is Well Prepared For A Purpose Driven Retirement." Forbes. March 21, 2013. https://www.forbes.com/sites/robertlaura/2013/03/21/pastor -rick-warren-is-practicing-what-he-preaches-and-getting-ready-f or-retirement/?sh=1e3f63744dbf.

3. Ibid

My journey through *The Purpose-Driven Life* has given me a God-centered focus as I find personal answers to the question, "What on earth am I here for?" Consider asking this same question of yourself and turn to God for the answer. His response may surprise you. One thing is certain: He wants to use you to bless others.

PLANNING YOUR ENCORE

- Does life in the Encore Season find you searching for a new purpose?

- Make a list of your interests, passions, and skills.

- How can you find an intersection of those three lists to plan activities that excite and inspire you?

Being successful and fulfilling your life's purpose are not at all the same thing: You can reach all your personal goals, become a raving success by the world's standard, and still miss the purpose of your life.
—Pastor Rick Warren

Chapter 6

Education Encore

Education is the key to unlocking the world, a passport to freedom.
—Oprah Winfrey

There's a name in higher education used to describe an older student returning to college or starting college after being away for several years or even decades—"a nontraditional."

Nontraditional, but certainly not uncommon.

GRAYING OF COLLEGE CAMPUSES

According to a *Forbes* article from 2018, a majority of college students are not those who have come directly from high school.[1] I doubt this trend has reversed.

Expanded access to higher education means older students don't have to live in dorms or fraternity/sorority houses.

---

1. "Going Back To College After 50: The New Normal?" Forbes. Next Avenue, July 1, 2018.
   https://www.forbes.com/sites/nextavenue/2018/07/01/going
   -back-to-college-after-50-the-new-normal/#5667504131ff.

Online learning opportunities have exploded in recent years, creating an affordable and accessible way for men and women to return to the classroom, even a virtual classroom, without disrupting their entire lives. During the Coronavirus Pandemic of 2020, many colleges and universities were forced to offer most, sometimes all, courses online, creating expanded opportunities for distance learning for years to come.

Why are there so many later-in-life college students? A wide variety of reasons can be a motivation for returning to the classroom, like learning a new skill set or trying to get a leg up in an evolving industry. But sometimes the joy of learning can be its own motivator!

The *Forbes* article outlines four key reasons people over fifty decide to return to the classroom as a student:

1. Prepare for a Second Career

After spending an entire career in the workforce, earning a living, and raising a family, there are often passions and interests those entering the Encore Season can develop and use in a second-act career. This could be the time to pursue a more meaningful path—perhaps something in social services or education. Organizations in the non-profit world are always looking for experienced leadership. Sometimes, a shift in a career strategy might require going back to school.

2. Stay Competitive in the Workforce

Staying up-to-date and competitive is especially important in the case of technology-focused fields, where quickly evolving systems, like computer hardware or software, can create a circumstance where an older adult can find themselves passed over for opportunities or promotions in favor of a younger person who is keeping up with the changes and expertise. Going back to school, even taking a few classes regularly, can allow an older person to stay more competitive in their current field.

3. Grow through Challenges and Learn New Things

Have you always wanted to learn a language? Or become more technologically proficient? Earn that advanced certification? There are lots of degreed and non-degreed opportunities available in the twenty-first century. Online classes make it possible to connect to programs in just about every field of study, and they are often offered at lower costs, or even free.

4. Meet a Long-Held Goal

Returning to school can be the motivator for someone who always wanted to earn a degree but got off track somewhere along the way.

COGNITIVE CONNECTIONS

In-person classrooms allow us to create new connections with classmates and become part of small study groups. These groups allow for more in-depth exploration of the material covered in the classroom, energetic conversations about the subject, and how it may relate to current events. This opportunity to engage in discussions with new people will help create intellectual and emotional connections. Taking a few classes at either a community college or local university is often a great way to surround yourself with like-minded classmates who will help you find inspiration and excitement while producing a bit of a challenge.

You will have a reason to get up in the morning and a reason to stay off the couch and turn off the TV in the afternoon and evening. But don't forget about the homework! You'll have to study and write papers.

Getting (or finishing) that degree doesn't even have to be the end goal. Increasing knowledge, finding a challenge, and creating new relationships are great reasons to take the leap and head back to school.

PLANNING YOUR ENCORE

- Did you finish your college degree? Would you like to get an advanced degree? How about learning a foreign language? Think about what you could study that would excite or motivate you and write out some goals!

- Even if there is not much of a monetary pay-off, which educational aspirations have you always wanted to explore? Learning to trade stocks? The skills to be a social worker? Diving into new art mediums or art history? List anything that interests you.

- Think back to your Growing Up season and what your dream job was at that time. What skills or knowledge would you have to attain to reach that goal?

It's never too late to be what you might have been.
—George Elliot

Chapter 7

Create a Career Encore

In the world of business, the people who are most successful are those who are doing what they love.
    —**Warren Buffett**

Regardless of the work we are doing, in the Encore Season, we *must* avoid doing it just because it was always what we did or were trained to do.

Is this the time when we step away from the corporate world and work for a nonprofit?

For someone who has always had a job in one place, is this the time to consider taking a position that will involve more travel?

For someone who has always worked in a big corporate setting, is this the time to move to a smaller organization?

Or for someone who always has been in a small organization, is this the time to step into corporate America?

For stay-at-home moms, is this the time to step into the workforce, using all the skills you learned while running the small corporation known as a household?

Is this the time to start your own business?

VOCATIONAL SECOND (OR THIRD) ACT

AARP is an organization for people fifty and up. According to an AARP report, for a majority of Americans, retirement barely exists anymore[1]. Some older Americans keep working out of financial necessity, but many others work because it keeps them connected and fulfilled.

As we remain more active in our later years, most of us will have more time to spend on a career "re-boot." AARP supports a special program called Encore[2] that helps older adults find meaning and purpose in life. Encore dates to the late '90s and was developed because of considerable interest from people looking to find a new position or path in life after stepping away from what had been a decades-long career. Most of those interested in encore careers were looking to work fewer than thirty hours a week.

The Encore Career Handbook, written by Marci Alboher, states that even if an older worker doesn't get paid, they want to remain connected, relevant, useful, and engaged. These are feelings similar to

---

1. Cramer, Bill. "Ready for Your Second Career?" Work and Jobs. AARP, September 27, 2013. https://www.aarp.org/work/working-after-retirement/info-10-2013/ready-for-your-second-career.html.

2. Homepage. CoGenerate (Formerly Encore), Accessed May 22, 2023. https://cogenerate.org/.

what someone wishing to transition into an Encore Season career may have felt in that "we're not done yet."[3]

The idea here is to figure out if there is a professional dream you may have been holding and not waste time deciding if it's worth pursuing. The associate state director for AARP Michigan, Jennifer Feuerstein, says, "Deciding what you want to do when you 'grow up' can be overwhelming. So really consider what your dream job would be and why. Asking 'the why' is critical. As you explore your encore career path, you may decide you want to phase into retirement instead of going 'cold turkey.' This could include cutting back hours or taking on a new role with fewer responsibilities. The best part is that you get to explore and try new things. And if it doesn't work, you're in the stage of life where you can make changes."

If you have always been an employee and never a manager, but you have those leadership desires, is this the time to apply for a managerial position?

Or is this the time in life to start your own business?

AARP's Feuerstein says entrepreneurs who launch and build a business in the second half of life—over age fifty—are one of the fastest-growing groups of business owners. Research from the Small Business Administration shows one in four individuals ages forty-four to seventy are interested in becoming entrepreneurs. If you fall into that category and don't know where to start, check out AARP's Work For Yourself@50+, which provides support and information to help you get started.

"Finding your encore career begins with asking 'what's my next?' Sometimes you know exactly what you want to do. Sometimes the

---

3. Alboher, Marci. 2010. The Encore Career Handbook. New York: Workman Publishing Company.

answer isn't so clear. The idea of an encore is saving the best for last. And this is your opportunity to carve out the late-stage career that you really desire," says Feuerstein.

PLANNING YOUR ENCORE

- Instead of retiring completely from the workforce, would you like to make a career change?

- If you spend much of your adult life as a stay-at-home parent, is this the time to take your incredible skill set into the workforce?

- Have your last several years at work left you feeling drained or unfulfilled? Is there a job or career field that would fill you with excitement and energy? Describe what an encore career would entail and how you would feel once you make this change.

You are never too old to set another goal or dream a new dream.
—**C. S. Lewis**

Chapter 8

Encore Season Hobbies

Find three hobbies you love: One to make you money, one to keep you in shape, and one to be creative.

—Anonymous

When we were raising our children and working in our chosen vocations, we rarely had the extra time or resources to explore a creative outlet for ourselves. *Heck, I barely had time to fold clothes or empty the dishwasher.* However, we created myriad opportunities for our children to explore their hobbies, investing our time, money, and energy into their interests over the years.

Transitioning into the Encore Season gives us many more open hours in our weeks, and for some of us, it provides extra resources.

It's time to explore some options you may have never considered in the past. I discovered a great example of this when I was invited to produce a painting for a benefit art auction. I never thought of myself as having any artistic ability. But the organizers of this event paired me with a wonderful elementary school art teacher, who happened to be a friend of mine: Kathleen Broekhuizen. She is married to my daughter's former high school soccer coach (who is spending his Encore Season running a faith-based organization for teens after retiring from his career as a high school guidance counselor).

It turns out Kathleen is quite a talented coach in the world of watercolor painting. In the style of Bob Ross, she coached me through creating a landscape watercolor. I would never have imagined I would be able to create! Because of this experience, I am looking forward to exploring more outlets for my imagination and art.

But striking a chord in my previously undiscovered art gene has led me to dig deeply about other things I would love to learn, or at least *try to learn!*

Here's my Top 10 list:

- Learn to juggle.

- Learn to play the piano.

- Learn to sew.

- Learn to make fabric bows for gift baskets.

- Learn to solve the Rubik's Cube.

- Explore my newly discovered artistic skills.

- Improve my golf skills.

- Improve my tennis skills.

- Join a bowling league.

- Add yoga to my wellness routine.

PLANNING YOUR ENCORE

- Is there an interest or passion you have not pursued because you did not have the time or resources in the other seasons of your life?

- Is there something you remember doing with great passion in your Growing Up or Young Adult seasons? Would you be interested in trying that again today?

- Who do you know who could help you develop your interest or passion? Try writing your Top 10 list. The Encore Season allows us the opportunity to pursue some of those hobbies. Make the most of it!

To be really happy and really safe, one ought to have at least two or three hobbies, and they must all be real.
—Winston Churchill

Chapter 9

Serving Others in the Encore Season

Life's most persistent and urgent question is, what are you doing for others?
—**Dr. Martin Luther King Jr.**

There is a common phrase associated with doing something for someone else. "You get more out of it than you ever put in." This is the case in any volunteer effort, especially during the Encore Season.

FIGHTING BOREDOM

A blank calendar can seem more daunting than the jam-packed days and over-scheduled chaos that was the Juggling Act's cornerstone. The gaping holes in the daily to-do lists can almost trigger a return to the familiar lament of "I'm bored," which is often played on a repeat cycle by kids and teens. "What is there to do?"

BOOSTING PHYSICAL AND MENTAL HEALTH

The benefits of volunteering include reducing stress, improving mood, and preventing loneliness. A volunteer experience can help an individual entering the Encore Season create new social connections. As I shared earlier, it was through volunteering that I found an enduring friendship with my dear friend, Christy. Volunteering also helps reduce the risk of developing physical ailments, like high blood pressure, by keeping participants more active and engaged.

HELP WANTED

One of the most significant issues in the Encore Season is feeling like we may have nothing to contribute or that nobody needs us. Every community has hundreds of organizations that rely on volunteer help. Those special skills developed and honed through decades in the workforce could be put to great use in hospitals or schools.

Wondering how to get connected? Do a Google search of volunteer opportunities in your community, specifying any areas you are interested in helping.

- Love animals? Contact the animal shelter.

- Love to read? Contact a school or library.

- Love babies or small children? Contact a hospital or child-care center.

- Love nature and the outdoors? Contact your county's parks department.

- Want to fill the nest? Consider becoming a foster parent.

You've been giving your best to your employer and your family; now is an opportunity to share your best with others. You have so much to give your community! Volunteering can bring a sense of purpose and fulfillment and help create new relationships simultaneously.

PLANNING YOUR ENCORE

- Do you have a passion for a certain organization, project, or cause? How can you devote your new freedom to helping improve life for others?

- Do you have a unique passion or area of expertise that could help society?

- Take out a notebook and write down five specific causes you might like to serve or get involved with. Make a plan to reach out; then get connected and serve!

What is the essence of life? To serve others and to do good.
—Aristotle

Chapter 10

Getting Healthier in the Encore Season

It is health that is the real wealth, not pieces of gold and silver.
—Mahatma Gandhi

The Encore Season is a great time to focus on our physical health.

For many of us, the Juggling Act season involved providing plenty of opportunities for our kids to be physically fit. Our aerobic activities may have consisted of shivering in the bleachers of our youngsters' sporting events during inclement weather or doing battle with the steering wheel while driving another leg of the carpool.

Neglecting our commitment to healthy living for years (or decades) has come from sacrifice. From late nights with the kids to early-morning alarm clocks for meetings and tasks at work, just a few of the personal physical sacrifices may have included:

- Sleep.

- Physical exercise.

- Nutritious meals.

While we were in our twenties, thirties, and maybe forties, we may have short-changed our health without always noticing the impact. The Encore Season has us shifting through our fifties, sixties, and beyond, where the signs of aging are becoming easier to see and feel.

The Encore Season is a time when caring for our bodies can and should become a greater priority. This transition gives us the time, resources, and energy to take better care of ourselves!

I've gone through streaks of exercise in my life. I've never really been a runner, but I did train for a 5K for the first time when my youngest was in middle school. The effort was to prepare for our school's version of a Girls on the Run program. I made it through the training because I had a buddy who was about the same running level as I was at the time (read "couch potato" here). It was ironic because her daughter ended up running cross country, and my daughter was a successful all-around athlete at the same age.

We moms were happy just driving the girls to where they needed to be, grabbing a cappuccino from the gas station, and then sitting at practice chatting while we watched the girls go through their training. As I look back on that time, I think it would've been a great time to have just grabbed a bottle of water and our walking shoes and spent the hour or so while the girls were at practice getting in a bit of physical activity. But of course, when we were younger, in our thirties and forties, we weren't motivated to put in the effort. Plus, it was easy to find excuses because of the exhausting schedules we kept.

GOAL ACCOMPLISHED

I was so proud of us when we finished the 5K. My goal at the time was to not walk. The girls went at their own pace. My daughter Jenn passed me on the course. She was finishing her second mile as I was finishing my first. She was booking it! After she finished the race, she ran the last mile with me, probably logging five miles herself that day.

That was the only 5K I ran that year. Looking back on that time, I wish I would have stayed engaged with running or jogging. Doing the physical work to get to the point where I could do the 5K, even though I wasn't breaking any land speed records, was the hard part. If I would've just dedicated myself to running a mile and a half three times a week, I could have kept myself in better shape.

Fast-forward to the year my youngest was graduating from high school. It was a pivotal year, as she was moving away to college and leaving the nest much emptier than it'd ever been. I'd become close with one of the moms on her AAU basketball team, a lady whose daughter was Jenn's roommate. Her nest was emptying at the same time as mine. She is a few years younger than me and also more dedicated to fitness than I was. We made a pact that year that we would sign up and run several 5K events. There are multiple reasons this was a great strategy.

First, most of these happen on Saturday mornings, which are hard mornings for the newly empty nesters. When our girls were living at home and in school, Saturday mornings were busy with school sports or AAU, so to suddenly wake up without obligations made it a very painful time of the week for us.

There is such a social aspect of running in a 5K due to race event camaraderie. Besides the physical fitness benefits of running, there is the physical rush of endorphins from working out. A sense of community comes from being surrounded by people looking to connect and engage with people also trying to take better care of themselves.

That year I ran nine 5Ks!

For the next couple of years, I only ran a couple of 5Ks and switched my active time from running to biking.

Now I have settled on walking as my favorite activity. I have a personal goal of walking at least 10,000 steps every day. I keep track using a Fitbit since my personality has a competitive side and is motivated by setting and hitting daily goals. Much of the time, I put my iPhone in my fanny pack and listen to my favorite podcast on a solo adventure. I will still occasionally meet up with a friend or invite my husband along for the journey too. During the cold and snowy season in West Michigan, a local shopping mall replaces sidewalks and nature trails as my adventure route. Mall walking is a great activity for the Empty Nest season, though it's a good idea to leave the credit cards at home!

The bottom line is being physically active is crucial in this stage of our lives. It is important to keep our bodies moving, maintain our muscle tone, and engage our cardiovascular system. It's also essential for bone health and has mental health benefits, especially when we engage in outside activities.

PLANNING YOUR ENCORE

- How do you feel physically? Do you have regular aches and pains? Do you get tired quickly while engaging in simple activities?

- Is there an activity or exercise routine you could commit to doing regularly?

- Is there someone you could commit to meeting with regularly who would motivate you to become more physically active? Reach out to that person TODAY!

Nothing matters more than your health. Healthy living is priceless. What millionaire wouldn't pay dearly for an extra ten or twenty years of healthy aging?
—Peter Diamandis

SECTION 3: Encore Surroundings

A house is made of walls and beams; a home is made of hopes and dreams.

—Unknown Author

Chapter 11

Is It Time to Sell Your "Forever Home?"

Are you going to Love It or are you going to List It?
—Hilary Farr & David Visentin

There is a television show I love called *Love It or List It*. Hilary Farr is a classy, talented interior designer, and David Visentin is a spunky, funny real estate agent. The two embark on an episode-by-episode competition to help families decide about their housing situations.

Each family profiled during an episode is no longer satisfied with their current house. In most cases, the house is too small or doesn't function properly, needing more than just an aesthetic makeover. Essentially, the family has decided their nest is no longer the right fit. The family gives each designer a budget, a list of required items, and the spaces that must be changed or improved for that house to continue to serve the family's needs in the present and into the future. One designer works with the current home. The other designer, the real estate agent, works to find a new home that fits the requirements.

In most episodes, viewers learn the family moved into the house during a different life season. Gradually, year by year, circumstances changed. The family grew by having more children or because their children got older and bigger, and the needs and tastes of the family changed. Growth was just one of a variety of reasons for the hunt for change.

As Hilary works through the list of changes, the current home is transformed. The challenge is that one major thing that can't change is the square footage. The house is transformed into a more workable space, even though the overall size remains the same. The other thing that can't change is the location of the home. In real estate, there's a phrase: "It's all about location, location, location!" No matter what the remodel does to the home, the location is what it is, for better or for worse.

While the designer and construction team transform the family's home, the other host, David, takes the family on tours of potential new homes. He shows the family houses that are move-in ready and that "check all the boxes" on the family's wish list. The new homes already have the right number of bedrooms and bathrooms, an updated kitchen, and, often, an open floor plan, along with perhaps the most suitable backyard or preferred garage. It is a turnkey solution to giving the family everything it has identified on that list of what they want in a living space. Sometimes, the new home is in a different neighborhood or a different location, which may or may not present an objection with the family. At the end of the journey, the family tours their current home, with the completed renovations. They wrestle with their choices, then the designer asks, "Are you going to love it?" and the realtor asks, "Or are you going to list it?" As they cut to commercial, audiences are left to wonder *will the family stay put, or will the family pack up their boxes and move to that new space?*

The decision becomes emotional along the way, especially for families looking to leave a home they have lived in for many years, where they experienced significant life changes. Maybe they brought babies home into that house from the hospital, or maybe it was their first home. They may have watched their children grow up there or battled conflict and stood the test. An attachment to that house is an essential part of their story.

As we transition into the Encore Season, it might be time to think about changing our living environment. Aside from occasional visits from out-of-town adult children (and maybe grandchildren), our current home may boast too many bedrooms and bathrooms. It might be out-of-date and need remodeling, or perhaps it no longer suits your current style. Maybe your home is in a rural area and your "Encore" spirit would love to live in a downtown condo.

An emotional attachment to my surroundings often seems to be the deciding factor for considering moving or staying put. Maybe you feel this way too. Moving out of the home where your children grew up feels like moving away from the memories. And while I don't believe in ghosts, I can close my eyes and picture my children opening presents under the tree in our great room on Christmas morning, bounding through the front door with excitement after making the varsity team, or answering the door to find a high school crush on the front porch with the "prom-posal." Occupying the same space where these memories took place somehow keeps those memories alive and fresh.

But does it really?

As my transition into the Encore Season unfolds, I'm finding it easier to let go of the need to physically occupy the same space where all those incredible memories happened. Time has made a way for me to focus on what I want. I have begun to reflect on a more personal list of questions about my living environment:

- Do I need all this space? Or would I prefer a smaller space?

- Do I want to keep living in the same location?

- Do I want to live in a more urban setting?

- Would I prefer a condo or a house in this stage of life?

- Am I willing to keep spending as much time on the cleaning and upkeep of my nest?

- Would changing my living environment make it easier to focus on the future?

When I watch *Love It or List It*, I have typically rooted for the people on the show to stay with their current (but now updated) home, mainly because of all the memories that happened there. As my Encore Season continues, I'm finding it easier to imagine the benefits for the people on the program (and even myself) of making a different choice. Moving into a new space does not erase the memories of the Juggling Act season. A move may even allow for fresh memories to come more easily.

Oh, and if you chose it, moving brings one additional blessing—the knowledge that another family will get to spend their Juggling Act years in the home that was such a warm and comfortable place for raising your family.

No matter what you choose, a home that fits your season of life makes that season all the better.

PLANNING YOUR ENCORE

- Think about your dream living space. Are you ready to downsize or right-size? Are you ready to ditch suburbia for a downtown condo? Would you like to move from a neighborhood to the country? Go from a house to a condo? Do you prefer rural or urban? Ever dream of living waterfront?

- Do you know anyone who could help you make a decision about changing your nest? Reach out to that person for a conversation and start exploring your options. There's no harm in looking!

- Plan a vacation (or even just an overnight or weekend getaway) and stay in a rental property that would allow you to experiment with the lifestyle in your "dream surroundings."

If we were meant to stay in one place, we'd have roots instead of feet.
—Rachel Wolchin

Chapter 12

Climate Change in the Encore Season

When I no longer thrill to the first snow of the season, I'll know I'm growing old.

—Lady Bird Johnson

It's confession time. I hate cold weather. I dislike snow. And I don't like ice.

The irony, of course, is that as a television meteorologist in a northern climate, I've spent decades forecasting snow and ice with a smile on my face! For a few short years, when I was in preschool and kindergarten, my family lived in Missouri—not exactly the tropics but at least warmer than across the northern states. So, aside from a brief stint during a part of my life I can barely remember, almost every state I have lived in shares a border with Canada! I was born in New Jersey. After kindergarten, we moved to Montana. Of course, I did not have any say in that matter.

But the choices that followed were all mine. I hopscotched across the country during my college years. From Montana, I moved west to attend Washington State University for two years. I then moved east to Wisconsin, where I finished my first degree and began my professional career. After a few years in Wisconsin, I took a position for a brief period in South Dakota before moving to Michigan to climb another rung on the television news ladder.

At each career crossroads, I had a decision to make about where to plant myself for the next chapter of my life. The television news business works a little like professional sports. You start in smaller markets to gain a year or two of experience and then move to progressively bigger markets until you reach the network or a market where you decide to put down roots and live your life. This was the case back in the 1980s and '90s, though with today's world of online reporting and digital technology, moving up or down by several market sizes at a time is easier. Back then, to get a new position, a personality would make a videotape of several of their best segments and mail it to hiring news directors. Applying at each station was an individual proposition, so a candidate could look for a position in any geographic area in the country.

NORTHERN GIRL

For me, living in a northern climate was almost all I had known. I applied at stations several hundred to a couple thousand miles away from where I was living (or where my parents were living). Yet it seemed only logical for me to apply to television news jobs in the northern part of the United States.

When I took the position in Michigan, I did not know I would make this the final market stop in my career. I would spend the next thirty-plus years in that same TV market. Even though I changed jobs after finishing my certification as a meteorologist and changed stations from CBS to the NBC affiliate in the market, I stayed planted in the same place for most of my television career.

WINTER DISTRACTIONS

For much of the year, I love the climate in Michigan. From late spring through summer and into late fall, the weather, on average, ranges from beautiful to tolerable.

It's only the unseasonably cold days of spring and fall and the bitter days of winter that I cannot stand. Getting through that part of the year while my nest was full was manageable. As a parent of three busy athletes, there was always a lot to do and many activities, which provided ample distractions. All three of my kids played hockey, which was an absolute blast to watch! And my youngest filled our winter months with basketball.

LONG, COLD WINTER

It's only now that all the sports and other activities are over that living in the northern climate seems almost unbearable.

When the icy winds blow and it's impossible to get outside to do any of the activities I love, like walking, biking, and playing golf, I regret the decision not to plant myself some place warmer.

GETTING A SOUTHERN NEST

In your Encore Season, do you dream of regularly escaping the long, cold winters? A seasonal climate change may be what you need to help break the ice.

Of the fifty states, there is one I have fallen in love with most: Florida. Besides the promise of the "sunshine state" filling my life with bright and warm weather year-round, my sweet baby grandsons live in Tampa.

Perhaps there is another locale for you to check out too. Try to visit some place with a different climate and a different pace of life. If your grandkids live there, then perhaps the easier the decision will become!

PLANNING YOUR ENCORE

- What climate do you want to live in? Is it too cloudy where you live? Is it too cold? Too warm? Are you ready to become a snowbird? Describe your dream locale in detail.

- Write down the steps you would have to take to spend time in a dream location regularly.

- What is a realistic timeline for making it a reality?

You have brains in your head. You have feet in your shoes.
You can steer yourself in any direction you choose.
You're on your own. And you know what you know.
And YOU are the one who'll decide where to go . . .
—Dr. Seuss, *Oh, the Places You'll Go*

SECTION 4:
Encore
Relationships

As you get older, you really just want to be surrounded by good people. People that are good for you, good to you, and good for your soul.
   —The Minds Journal

Chapter 13

Friendships in the Encore Season

We have three types of friends in life: friends for a reason, friends for a season and friends for a lifetime.
—Author Unknown

Friendships fall into many categories. Certain friends come and go from our lives in different stages and different settings. Some friendships are new. Others are enduring.

Think of the blessings of friendship as falling into one or more of these *C* Categories:

- Connection

- Communication

- Casual

- Consistent

- Community

- Companionship

- Compassion

- Counsel

- Commonality

- Cheerleader

Even though friendships often play a significant role in our social life, friendships can also impact our health and well-being. According to research conducted by the Mayo Clinic[1], good friends are good for our health. During the good times in life, friends help us find joy and celebrate the good times. Trusted friends are valuable in providing comfort and support during difficult times. The most special friends are the people we can't wait to share our good news with and cry with during times of sadness, loss, and pain. Friends keep us company, prevent loneliness, and allow us to do the same for them.

Friends can also:

- Increase our sense of belonging and purpose.

- Boost our happiness and reduce stress.

- Improve our self-confidence and understand our worth.

- Help us cope with traumas, such as divorce, serious illness, job loss, or the death of a loved one.

- Encourage us to change or avoid unhealthy lifestyle habits, such as excessive drinking or a lack of exercise.

---

1. Article written by Mayo Clinic staff, dated August 24, 2019, www.mayoclinic.org.

Dionne Warwick famously created an anthem about these special relationships in her 1980s hit song "That's What Friends Are For."

CHOOSING OUR FRIENDS

It's commonly believed that we take on the values, traits, and character of the five people with whom we spend most of our time. During the Young Adult and Juggling Act seasons, much of our time was spent with people we may never willingly choose as companions—whether they were the parents of our children's friends or teammates or fellow employees at our place of business. As we transition to the Encore Season, the activities that fill our schedules, and thus our lives, can be those of our choosing. So, too, regarding friendships. No longer are we forced to maintain friendships originally chosen by proximity or team colors, not by mutual mascots or paychecks. This is the time in life when we can make friends based on the common interests we might share.

People inspire you or they drain you. Pick them wisely.
—Hans F. Hansen

FRIENDSHIPS ON DISPLAY

There is a series of TV shows on Bravo TV called *The Real Housewives*. The shows feature groups of women in several major cities.

They started in Orange County, California, and promoted it as a reality TV show that would chronicle the relationships and life adventures of a group of high-profile, uber-wealthy, successful women who are friends or in the same circle of friends. Some individual relationships are closer than others, with some women in the group considered only acquaintances of one another and others being intimate friends.

From the initial show in the Los Angeles area, the series spread to include different communities across the country, featuring high-profile, successful women in each location.

As of 2019, more than a dozen cities feature *Real Housewives* spin-offs, from *The Real Housewives of New York City* to *The Real Housewives of Beverly Hills* and from *The Real Housewives of New Jersey* to *The Real Housewives of Atlanta*. There is even *The Real Housewives of Salt Lake City*. There are international versions of the shows spanning from Vancouver to Melbourne and Athens. Lots of glamour, money, and drama!

Even though marketed and promoted as reality TV, it is difficult to believe genuine relationships would contain the explosive emotional drama and fireworks as those chronicled in these programs. It's my experience that real friendships don't melt down into public screaming matches, name-calling, or back-biting, the likes of which take center stage during each episode. It's hard to imagine behaving in such a way toward people, especially those who are in our social circles or friend groups.

As the shows continue to air, season to season, cameras follow these women through the many extremes in their lives. Some are getting married; some are filing for divorce. Some are having babies, and some are watching their children grow up and move away. Some battle substance abuse, and others are arrested.

Through these challenging times, when it appears these women need the support of a good friend, the cameras and producers don't always showcase these relationships in a positive light—what it means to be a loyal friend. Of course, the ratings may not be as good if these women were having coffee, going to Bible study, playing cards or golf, and supporting one another in positive ways!

So the drama continues, the cameras keep rolling, and millions of people watch it all unfold.

Perhaps it is best served as a cautionary tale for all of us who are in relationships with people, either casual or close. How we treat people impacts how they think, act, and feel. We have a real opportunity to treat others with kindness and compassion and to be supportive and loving in every relationship in our lives.

REALITY? TV

While my sincere hope is *The Real Housewives* series is not displaying *reality*, there are valuable lessons to be learned regarding genuine friendship.

Indeed, the mark of character is how we behave when we believe nobody is watching, which might be why these women carry on in such callous, dramatic, and contemptuous ways in front of the cameras. Those relationships will only survive if there is true love, caring, and compassion when the bright lights stop shining.

Indeed, no matter how much money someone has, how beautiful their home may be, or how glamorous they may appear, we each need to develop friendships that lift us instead of tear us down. We are social creatures and can only be at our best when we choose friendships and relationships that inspire us to be better versions of ourselves.

LITERARY FRIENDS

I kept always two books in my pocket: one to read, one to write in.
—**Robert Louis Stevenson**

Different people come into our lives in different seasons, especially as we transition from one stage in life to another. With the free time I discovered after my youngest child moved away to college, I became determined to reach for a dream I'd been harboring for at least four decades, the dream of writing a book. I'm in good company with this dream; an article by Justine Tal Goldberg on the website Publishing Perspectives presents Joseph Epstein's research that suggests 81 percent of Americans want to write a book.

That's two hundred *million* people!

Why don't more people write that book? Perhaps it's a lack of time, ambition, confidence, or know-how. I used many of those perceived barriers as excuses for why I had not chased my literary dream. Like many want-to-be authors, I had talked about my goal so often that for Christmas one year, my son Jacob and daughter-in-law Taylor bought me the specialized author software package Scrivener for my home computer!

So how did I turn that decades-long dream into the pages you are reading? By developing relationships with a group of extraordinary people who have come into my life over the past several years. They mentored and inspired me as I reached for my dream of becoming a published author.

MY FIRST AUTHOR FRIEND

God brings certain people into our lives to serve as special inspirations, and Cindy Bultema is that person in my life. I got to know Cindy a couple years ago when she stepped away from her successful career as an author, speaker, and thought leader in the women's Christian inspirational space to take over the role of executive director for an important Christian ministry for young girls called GEMS. GEMS stands for Girls Everywhere Meeting the Savior. I'm thinking about lobbying Cindy to start a similar organization for people in the Encore Season called Grandparents Everywhere Meeting the Savior. (Could this be GEMS 2.0?)

Cindy and I connected as she was taking over her new role. She asked me to help with some remarkable new initiatives she was starting within this organization. Interestingly, my daughters had both been GEMS growing up, and I was even a GEMS leader in our church at one point. In my meeting with Cindy, we talked about this great organization, and I picked her brain about her life as an author and speaker. I shared my lifelong desire to become an author, and she became a wonderful mentor and prayer partner as she encouraged me to reach for my dream.

It would take me a couple of years to gain the confidence to start writing my first book. Still, occasional meetings with Cindy gave me the motivation and inspiration I needed to believe I had an important message to share with women walking through the same stage in life I was experiencing.

Cindy's important message to me was that she wrote books aimed at helping women through different times in their lives; many were Christian devotional books. Her life as a speaker allowed her to travel to conferences and workshops and serve as a teacher, counselor, coach, and cheerleader. Cindy's career was similar to the one I had been envisioning for me.

In her new role as GEMS leader, she also incorporated those wonderful aspects of her life and creativity into breathing new life into this crucial worldwide ministry. As a member of my literary network, I value her prayerful support and wisdom as I enter this new chapter in my life.

Seeking friendships with people who are already successful in an endeavor we would like to undertake is a valuable investment of our time into a positive relationship. Like me, you may be inspired to become an inspiration for other women.

A "NOVEL" FRIENDSHIP

I first met Tracy Brogan when she was in our studio to conduct research for a novella she was writing. She wanted behind-the-scenes information about the inner workings of a television station. One of her principal characters was a meteorologist who was working in the world of morning television. She came into the television station to job shadow, and we clicked.

Tracy writes romances and romantic comedies. Her first book has sold over one million copies worldwide, and she has had several more highly successful titles since then. She recently crossed the lifetime sales benchmark of three million books sold!

I found Tracy to be an inspiration because she had harbored dreams of becoming an author for many years before finally taking the leap to submit her first manuscript. She made me think I could do the same.

FROM INTERVIEW TO INSPIRATION

It has been more than a decade since Wade Rouse fanned my literary fire. Wade walked away from a lucrative career to begin his Encore Season trying to make writing his full-time occupation. As a guest on the eightWest couch, Wade's appearance was to promote his memoir *It's All Relative*. At the time, I found it amazing that a successful Random House-contracted author lived in Saugatuck, just one county away from me in West Michigan. Over the past decade, Wade has become a mentor and encourager. He continues to write best-selling novels under the pen name Viola Shipman (to honor his late grandmother). Wade's willingness to share his expertise and enthusiasm led me to believe I could become an author too. One of the most significant pieces of advice I received from Wade was the secret to successfully finishing the writing process. "Keep your butt in the seat!" Wade's advice was clever and funny, but it became a guiding truth as I worked to create this book. To actually finish something, I had to *sit down and do the work!*

LITERARY PART-TIMERS

I have also connected with an elite group of individuals who have written (or helped produce) books as they continued with successful careers. I'll never forget the admiration—and envy—I felt when people I *knew* had written and published books.

Cynthia: I was in the library and found the book *Small Business for Big Thinkers* staring at me. It was written by a woman I knew, Cynthia Kay, who was a communications expert with a successful video production, coaching, and event production business.

Rick: I was on vacation in Florida and opened my iPad to review emails and discovered a request from Rick Vuyst to write an endorsement to be included in his first book, *I Just Wet My Plants*. Rick ran a successful group of landscaping stores called Flowerland and had become the go-to expert for all things plants, landscaping, and flowers in West Michigan. Rick's green thumb and quick wit served him well as the host of a weekly radio show focused on helping people with their planting dilemmas. Rick is truly living his Encore Season now, after selling his Flowerland stores and setting out on new adventures.

Tommy: With a last name synonymous with great value in a steak dinner, Tommy Brann put the lessons he learned from a lifetime spent in the difficult restaurant industry into a book called *Mind Your Own Business: Lessons from a Hardworking Restaurateur.* I have since watched Tommy fulfill his Encore Season dream by becoming a member of the Michigan State Legislature.

Ginger: The honest life lessons from a former co-worker who has become a nationwide household name. Ginger Zee wrote her *New York Times* best-selling memoir, *Natural Disasters: I Cover Them. I Am One,* and her follow-up book, *A Little Closer To Home.* These books feature a candid and inspirational journey through Ginger's battle with mental health issues, substance abuse, and an abusive relationship. She is one of the most recognizable and respected people in America. Ginger has also written a series of adventure books for young girls designed to entertain and spark an interest in meteorology.

Tim: As the former Grand Valley State University athletic director, who turned this rural West Michigan college into a perennial NCAA Division II powerhouse, Tim Selgo penned *Anchor Up: Competitive Greatness the Grand Valley Way* before beginning his Encore Season. He stepped away from the GVSU Athletic Department to become an inspirational speaker, leader, and coach.

Buck: I developed an extraordinary literary relationship with a man who was decades ahead of me professionally—in every sense! He had been a television weatherman and talk show host (at my very same station) who connected with me when he was a guest on my show talking about a book *he* had just written. He was less than a decade away from celebrating the century mark and quickly became a special friend. We struck an immediate bond, joking that HE was ME, but without the lipstick and high heels! I confided in Buck that I had a dream of becoming an author and shared the beginning stages of my fledgling manuscript with him. He was the first person to read any of my writing! Without his support, critiques, and encouragement, I doubt I would have ever taken the leap to become a published author.

As I considered launching my literary career, I wondered how each of these people had written books and had them published! So I reached out to them for advice and counsel. While each author had a different journey, genre, and audience, the message I received from each of them was the same: *JUST GO FOR IT!*

When we are attempting to chase big dreams in the Encore Season, it's important to seek relationships with people who can inspire and guide us on the journey. In my life, these are key players who will inspire me and help me unlock the courage I need to work on my book. Even though our initial encounters were coincidental, the relationships we have developed are true blessings.

Writing a book is a difficult undertaking. Whether you write a book someday or not, you will be challenged by something new. Having trusted friends and advisors who have gone through this experience made it easier for me to navigate the hard times. Don't be afraid to seek people who will help you navigate your new experiences. Developing personal relationships with people who have already accomplished the dreams you have for yourself will make those goals seem more doable. Since writing a book had been a dream of mine for decades, I tended to put published authors on a pedestal. Getting to meet and become friends with these people who had already accomplished that milestone (many times over) made my dream seem possible. Building a relationship—truly knowing someone—might just be the first step you need to take in your journey of reaching a major life goal.

PLANNING YOUR ENCORE

- Take out a notebook and make a list of the people with whom you spend most of your time? Why are those people the recipients of your most precious resource (time)? Do these people lift you up? How do you positively impact their lives? How are your closest friends like-minded and supportive of you? Are there toxic relationships in your life that are no longer serving you? Which friends can you rely on to keep your secrets and confidences?

- How can you serve your friends this week?

- When it comes to Encore Season dreams, are there people you can reach out to who are already accomplishing the dreams or goals you have for yourself? Where could you find someone to point you on the road to reaching your dream?

Time and good friends are two things that become more valuable the older you get.
—Unknown

Chapter 14

Relationships with Adult Children

With grown children, we can look back at both our mistakes and what we did well with our parenting, having conversations with a greater degree of honesty than was possible before. In getting older themselves, our adult children may begin to comprehend the burdens and strengths we carried from our own.

—Wendy Lustbader

As we enter the Encore Season, emptier schedules may now give us the luxury of more free time to spend with our adult children. Perhaps we realize how quickly time has passed in the life cycle of our family, prompting us to want deeper connections with our children. The heart-breaking lyrics of the song "Cat's in the Cradle" by Harry Chapin tell the story of a busy career-focused man who misses out on his son's Growing Up season—missing his child's first steps and being too busy to play catch with his son.

It's challenging for a parent to navigate new relationship dynamics with adult children and welcome new family members as adult children get married and have children. With this transition, many of us get to wear new titles in this season of life: in-law and grandparent. With these new roles, we need to adjust to new rules and responsibilities.

As our adult children forge their paths in the twenty-first century, they may move away to pursue educational or professional opportunities. While we celebrate the transition they are making from the Growing Up to the Juggling Act season and admire their sense of adventure and ambition, physical distance can make it complicated and challenging to develop the deep relationships we would like to have with them as adults.

We miss seeing them every day but are proud we have raised them to follow their dreams and find their way to make a mark in the world. We may envy watching the adult children of our friends settle nearby in the same city or state, while our kids follow a destiny that takes them to a new part of the country or even the other side of the globe. We yearn to keep our families together because, sometimes, physical distance creates a difficulty as adult children move to new communities or even new states for education or career opportunities. Indeed, physical distance can lead to or even intensify an emotional separation.

EVOLVING RELATIONSHIPS

Whether your adult children live nearby or far away, perhaps the most delicate of all relationships as we get older are the relationships we have with them. Sometimes transitioning is entirely smooth sailing, where the adult child leaves the nest and builds their own life, developing a new type of relationship with their parents. This new adult-to-adult relationship may seem like adult children are developing a friendship with their parents. Perhaps your adult child will invite you to join in special outings with their friends or become your partner in a bowling or golf league. This is a special and magical evolution, marking the parent and child's continued connectedness while entering a fun new stage that can sometimes be celebrated as a peer-to-peer relationship.

However, in other cases, an adult child will look back on their growing-up years and feel as though they weren't the glory days. Growing up was tough. The stress of academics, extracurricular activities, friendships, peer pressure, and societal pressure might make some children look back at the Growing Up season through less than rose-colored glasses.

Raising a child involves setting rules, establishing boundaries, and providing structure and discipline with the hope that the child becomes a self-reliant, self-sufficient young adult. It's almost ironic to think the better the job we did during the Growing Up season as parents will translate into more independent grown adults who will seem to need us even less. Perhaps you feel this way too. We want to be needed by our adult children but feel conflicted or hurt by their need for independence.

The balance is never easy to achieve, resulting in some children looking back at their childhoods and believing they were an easy time, while others will look at the rules, structure, and discipline as harsh, unyielding, and unfair. As parents now try to create adult relationships with those adult children, a tug-of-war can sometimes ensue.

LOOKING BACK AT THE PAST

We all have our memories and versions of reality. An adult child may look back on their growing-up years and remember certain occasions when things didn't exactly go their way. A strong-willed child may remember those episodes as battles for control of a situation or relationship.

Sorting all this out can be challenging and sometimes painful. Trying to achieve new relationships with grown children can represent hurt feelings brought on by difficult, conflicted, or even buried memories of the Growing Up season. As parents, we must be willing to admit we may not have had all the answers, and occasionally, we may have done or said things our child found offensive or hurtful. That doesn't mean only saying "I'm sorry" or trying to convince your child they are wrong or not entitled to their feelings. Your adult child may find comfort if you take the time to listen and try to understand their painful memories. If you are interested in mending or moving the relationship forward, you will need to be sincere and authentic in your approach to these difficult conversations.

WALKING ON EGGSHELLS

In her book, *Walking on Eggshells*, Jane Isay traveled all over the country and interviewed dozens of parents and dozens of grown children, nearly seventy-five people in all[1]. Isay shares the tug-of-war stories of many relationships, where the adult child struggles to assert independence while the parents try to release the grip of control over the child. In her research, Isay discovered most adult children deeply love their parents but want us to respect them as adults.

---

1. Isay, Jane. 2005. Walking on Eggshells. Flying Dolphin Press.

"I was surprised to find that many people in their twenties and thirties were eager to tell me how much they worry about their relationship with their parents and how much time they spend puzzling over how to stay close and still be independent."[2]

Isay reported the process of separation to be challenging but offers the optimistic advice that "since adulthood lasts for decades, we have plenty of time to adjust and get it right."[3]

FAMILY COUNSELING

Sometimes, family dynamics don't improve with time. As adult children leave home and start their own families, the parent-child relationship does not evolve. If this is the case for you and your family, please consider seeking the help of a trained family counselor. A professional counselor provides an independent and unbiased view of difficult situations.

Just a caution: family counselors don't come equipped with magic wands. Working through challenging family issues will be difficult. The right counselor gives perspective and understanding and, with enough time and honesty, can help navigate painful family relationships. Even if the relationship with your adult children doesn't improve as quickly as you hope, a licensed counselor may help you become stronger emotionally and improve your mental wellness.

---

2. Ibid.

3. Ibid.

PLANNING YOUR ENCORE

- Describe your relationship with your adult child(ren). If you aren't satisfied with the relationship, what could you do to change the dynamic? Be specific.

- Ask your adult child(ren) to describe the relationship they want to have with you.

- How will the flexibility of the Encore Season help you navigate the best relationship with your adult child(ren)?

Something I have learned . . . how to not treat my grown kids and their spouses. Yes, granted, my children will always be babies in my eyes, but when they are grown adults with beliefs and values all their own, I have to be able to respect that. Though they may not follow what I feel to be right, having a lasting, loving relationship with my children, their spouses, and my grandchildren will be valued more in my heart than what I might believe to be right.

—Monica Lawrence

Chapter 15

Nanaville: The Best Part

There are really only two commandments of Nanaville: love the grand-children and hold your tongue.
    —Anna Quindlen, *Nanaville*

Nothing can prepare us for the emotions we feel when we become a grandparent, when our child has a child. When we hold our children for the first time, the emotion that swirls is an incredible feeling, but holding the child of your child in your arms is more precious than words can ever express.

The emotions flood in and you are overcome with love. Love for this new life and more profound love, respect, and admiration for your child, who has brought this new life into the world. There is also an unimaginable hope for this new life and their future. There is a feeling of mortality in knowing this child will have decades beyond those in which you exist. There is a feeling of nostalgia in feeling time has flown, from the moment the doctor placed your child in your arms to now.

A NEW ROLE

At the precise moment of their birth, you know you would lay down your life for this child and for your child who brought this new life into the world. But, at that precise moment, you may also realize these emotions you're feeling take a backseat. You are not the pilot, nor even the copilot, in this little one's life journey. You have a new role to fill, and like everything else about life with an adult child, this is a delicate balance to figure out. What will your role be in the life of this grandchild?

I am new to this part of the journey, so I don't have it all figured out yet. What I have tried to do is enjoy every precious moment I get with my sweet grandchildren and let their parents know I am available for anything they need at any moment. I even dropped everything and drove to the airport in a snowstorm with two hours' notice to hop on a plane to fly to Florida when my little grandson was sick. Due to work and higher education commitments, my daughter and her husband needed some help. I was blessed to have the flexibility that allowed this grandma to come to the rescue!

Yes, I would do anything for this life.

A big part of the transition into life in Nanaville includes keeping healthy boundaries. Boundaries are always so important. You want to make sure you are offering help without being pushy. Your role is to be supportive but not overbearing. Loving, but not possessive. You must learn that respecting your child's household rules is one of the truest ways a grandparent shows love. A supportive grandparent does not undermine the authority of the parents. You will help reinforce a critical life lesson for your grandchild about respecting authority. Lead by example and show that you respect the rules established by your adult children—even when it comes to bedtime and candy!

Enjoy the flood of love this new life brings into your life. Enjoy it and strengthen it by respecting the boundaries of your adult children. You will make a wonderful grandparent.

PLANNING YOUR ENCORE

- Are you lucky enough to be a member of the "Grandparent Club?" Who are your role models for being a grandparent?

- How will the Encore Season help you become a more engaged and involved grandparent?

- Close your eyes and imagine five years from now, then ten years, fifteen years, twenty years, and so on. What do you envision your role in the life of your grandchild to be?

Grandchildren are the dots that connect the lines from generation to generation.

—Lois Wyse

Chapter 16

An Encore Season Carol

"I wear the chain I forged in life," replied the Ghost. "I made it link by link, and yard by yard; I girded it on of my own free-will, and of my own free-will I wore it. Is its pattern strange to you?"

"Or would you know," pursued the Ghost, "the weight and length of the strong coil you bear yourself? It was full as heavy and as long as this, seven Christmas Eves ago. You have laboured on it since. It is a ponderous chain."

—Charles Dickens, *A Christmas Carol*

One of the most poignant stories that encourages us to examine how we're spending our life is the Charles Dickens classic *A Christmas Carol*. There have been many modern remixes of this story, using a modified plotline and modern-day references and actors, but the overall story remains unchanged.

Ebenezer Scrooge is a very wealthy man but a miser. His former partner, Jacob Marley, has passed away and comes back to visit Scrooge as a ghost, along with the spirits of Christmas Past, Christmas Present, and Christmas Yet to Come, taking Scrooge on a series of adventures.

The Spirit of Christmas Past takes Scrooge back in time. The Spirit of Christmas Present takes Scrooge through the present-day celebrations he is missing. Finally, the Spirit of Christmas Yet to Come takes Scrooge to the lonely ending of his life, should he continue to live as he has been.

One of the central characters affected by Scrooge's miserly life is a child, Tiny Tim, who is disabled and lives in a poor family. Tiny Tim's health and the entire family would benefit if Scrooge was more generous.

YOUR VERSION OF THE STORY

Imagine your version of this classic story. Try to imagine ghostly visits to your past, present, and future. Who is your Jacob Marley? Who is your Tiny Tim?

I have imagined my trip through this story, where I travel through my past, present, and future—from life after high school, into the present day, and then into the yet-to-come. My parents, especially my mom, represent the character Tiny Tim. A Spirit of the Past would take me to my life right after high school, when I was launching out of my parents' home and into adulthood. A visit to that time in my life makes my heart break over the fact I left without staying in close connection. As I enter the Encore Season, I'm overwhelmed with guilt at discovering how much my parents must have missed me and worried about me. This transition must have been even more difficult since there were no cell phones or social media, no texting, FaceTime, Facebook, Snapchat, or other apps.

The beauty of life is, while we cannot undo what is done, we can see it, understand it, learn from it and change so that every new moment

*is spent not in regret, guilt, fear or anger but in wisdom, understanding
and love.*

—Jennifer Edwards

GUILT

Guilt can be another one of those powerhouse emotions that becomes unbearable during the transitional time into the Encore Season.
We look back at those opportunities we didn't take or the circumstances where we could have done things differently.

- We feel guilty for not spending more time with our parents.

- We feel guilty that we did something other than the option
  that was right ahead of us.

- We feel guilty for losing touch with our sibling(s).

- We feel guilty for not appreciating the energy and chaos of
  the full house.

Hindsight is not 20/20. Reality shades the memories we have as we
look at those opportunities we wish we had in front of us today.

Unlike a casual game of golf, you do not get to take a Mulligan or
have a redo. You can't go back in time and make a different decision.
Even if you could go back in time, there are just as many chances you
would make the same decision all over again. When day after day after
day stretches into week after week after week, month after month after
month, and year after year after year after year, it is easy to feel guilty
for not scheduling more time with your parents and/or siblings. This
can be especially challenging if one of those precious family members
has already passed away.

It's important when we look back and feel such guilt about the choices we made that we remember the next important *G*-word:

GRACE

In the Bible, grace is a way to describe being pardoned for something, even when we were guilty of doing it. Author Anne Lamott wrote about grace: "I do not at all understand the mystery of grace—only that it meets us where we are but does not leave us where it found us." In our personal lives and looking back at the growing-up years, we need to give ourselves grace. Hindsight, they say, is perfect, but not when it comes to grace. We tend to beat ourselves up more in hindsight, and guilt becomes a much more overwhelming and much easier feeling to give into. But moving forward meaningfully with the next chapter, stage, and season of your life will require giving yourself grace. As the Bible teaches us, God extends grace to sinners; likewise, you can extend grace to yourself for decisions that have come and gone.

CLARITY ABOUT THE PRESENT

This time travel exercise may give you some perspective and clarity about what's happening now with your children. As I remember leaving my parents' home, it was only because of my ignorance of their feelings and emotions that I did not stay in closer touch with them. I was not looking to escape my parents as much as I was branching out to make my way in the world. The distance, physical and other, was not because I was pushing away from them; I was moving toward my way in life.

As I transition into my Encore Season, a walk down memory lane with my own Jacob Marley and spirit visitors allows a more complete understanding of the separation. This was especially helpful as my youngest graduated from college and started forging her path in life. Even though we have plenty of space at home, I supported her need for freedom and independence as she transitioned from college student to adult. It's so much easier as a parent to adjust to this reality when we fully embrace the idea that our child is not moving *away* from us; our child is moving *toward* his or her own life.

The Encore Season has also spurred me to circle back with my parents and my only sibling to schedule more time for activities with them. Life has come full circle. I now have the flexibility to reconnect with my "original family"—the people who have been with me through every season.

PLANNING YOUR ENCORE

- What do you remember about leaving home? What do you recall about your mother and father making the transition into their Encore Season? Did they seem excited or sad?

- How can your relationship change, improve, and deepen as you begin your Encore?

- If members of your original family have already passed away, practice forgiveness and give yourself grace.

Leaving home, in a sense, involves a second kind of birth in which we give birth to ourselves.
—Robert Neelly Bellah

Chapter 17

Four-Legged Friends

I have found that when you are deeply troubled, there are things that you get from the silent devoted companionship of a dog that you can get from no other source.

—Doris Day

I'm the first to admit I have never been a pet person, especially not a dog person. While they were growing up, my kids often begged me to get them a dog. The answer was always no for a variety of reasons:

- The nest was already full.

- The Juggling Act season seemed too overwhelming to even entertain the thought of getting a dog. Dogs are a lot of work!

- They are smelly and dirty.

- A dog can damage a house and leave hair (and other messy things) behind.

- Dogs also need companionship, and we were out of the house so much of the time.

I was *not* a dog person—until Hank came along.

My daughter Jenn adopted Hank after she graduated from college. She was looking for a companion and was encouraged by a dog-loving friend to get a dog. I did not support this idea, but since she was a grown-up college graduate living outside the home, I did not have a say in this plan. I was also less than enthusiastic because Hank was not just a tiny puppy. He is half Great Dane and half mastiff-lab and considered a giant breed dog. To put it simply: full-grown Hank would easily weigh more than me!

Maybe you can see where this furry relationship is going. I have fallen in love with that dog. Hank is big but sweet. Occasionally, Jenn needs a pet sitter and asks me to watch him for a few hours or head over to her apartment and take him for a walk or let him out to go "potty."

As my relationship with Hank has grown (I now call him my "grand dog"), I have realized the great potential of having a four-legged friend to help fill the empty hours in the Encore Season.

An article by Kristen Sturt pointed out ten health benefits of having a dog, including improved heart health, boosting fitness and activity levels, improving social life, reducing stress, helping to stave off depression, helping to lose weight, and adding to a feeling of purpose.[1] Pets are so important to mental health that organizations match former members of the military with animals. Pets for Vets[2] and Pets

---

1. Sturt, Kristen. "The 10 Health Benefits Of Dogs (And One Health Risk)." What's Hot. Huff Post, September 23, 2016.

2. https://petsforvets.com/.

for Patriots[3] encourage pet adoption to provide a veteran with the companionship, responsibility, and love that comes from adopting a four-legged friend.

Having a pet can also help expand your social circle. With Hank around, I discovered the community that surrounds pet owners. This canine community includes fresh and friendly encounters at dog parks and along walking trails. People who have dogs are passionate about their animals and typically love meeting others with the same passion for their fur babies. Adding a dog to your life in this season can give you a sense of purpose and increase your social circle all at once.

If you are looking to add energy and a sense of purpose, perhaps a trip to the pet store or local animal shelter might be something to consider. It doesn't have to be a dog; a cat, hamster, Guinea pig, or even a goldfish can add new life to your home.

I have given thought to getting my own dog to help fill up my life, but having Hank in my life is almost like having another grandchild. I can enjoy him as much as I want, but when he needs to go potty in the middle of the night, it's Jenn who gets to take him out!

---

3. https://petsforpatriots.org.

PLANNING YOUR ENCORE

- If you have a pet, how has it helped you transition to the Encore Season?

- If you don't have a pet, how do you think it could help fill the empty space in your life?

- Can you think about people in your life who have a dog and might benefit from having your help in caring for their pet when life is busy for them?

A dog is the only thing on earth that loves you more than he loves himself.

—Josh Billings

Chapter 18

Enjoying "Alone Time" in the Encore Season

Loneliness is not a lack of company; loneliness is a lack of purpose.
 —Guillermo Maldonado

There is a lack of privacy that goes along with the child-raising years.

I have friends with little kids who say they can't even go to the bathroom or take a shower without little hands pounding on the door and yelling, "Mommy, are you in there?" It seems like those years are filled with "never alone" time. The lack of solitude and privacy can sometimes overwhelm a parent with little ones.

Fast-forward to the Empty Nest, and sometimes there is so much alone time that the silence and solitude can be overwhelming. For me, that was one of the hardest adjustments to make when I was emptying the nest.

I craved company.

I craved companionship.

I craved having someone around, even if we weren't talking!

I just love having someone else around. That's especially the case when that someone is a person I enjoy talking to, listening to, or just quietly hanging out with. There is a vast difference between being alone and being lonely. Loneliness is an emotional state—craving connection and feeling sad that nobody is there for that connection. Being alone is the physical state of just not being with somebody else. On the surface, the difference can seem subtle. In reality, the two concepts are vastly different. For me, however, those were the same things at the beginning of my Encore Season. I was physically alone, and emotionally, I was *lonely*!

Adjusting to the alone time involves finding enjoyable things to do by yourself. Depending on your mood and ambition level, these activities can be purpose-driven, inspirational, or just a mindless way to spend a few hours.

Here are just a few options I discovered:

- Reading fiction (entertainment).

- Reading non-fiction (education, inspiration).

- Watching Hallmark movies (There's always a happy ending!).

- Taking a walk.

- Binge-watching a Netflix show.

- Hopscotching through TED Talks on YouTube.

HOW AN OBSESSION LED TO ACTION

One of my favorite ways to spend my hours of independence is listening to podcasts. Almost by accident, I discovered this treasure trove of free programs on my iPhone. Many of these programs are fascinating and informative. I have gained inspiration and enthusiasm for taking on new projects by listening to people who are interested in the same things as me.

I may have never taken a leap of faith and written this book without discovering other authors and publishers who host podcasts. My newfound obsession turned into action for my Encore Season.

And, unlike many other things, listening to a podcast is usually a solo activity. I put on my headphones, grab my iPhone, call up the latest episode, and start walking. I feel less lonely while listening to great podcasts. The voices of the authentic people on the other side of my earbuds lit a fire in me to do my creative work. I liked what I heard so much that I started a podcast.

Maybe one day, you will look for a way to fill your quiet time, and you'll stumble upon my familiar voice. Regardless, look for podcasts, videos, and books that can help you as the voices of those strangers in "podcast land" helped me. Enjoy being alone by finding inspiration in new places.

PLANNING YOUR ENCORE

- How do you spend your alone hours right now?

- How would you describe the difference in your feelings when you are alone as opposed to those times when you are feeling lonely?

- Is there an activity you want to try—a personal goal or a hobby—that is best experienced by a party of one? Try searching YouTube, a podcast app, or your local library's online catalog for information about one of the hobbies you listed in the previous chapter. Look for something that inspires you to dig deeper into that subject.

I think it is very healthy to spend time alone. You need to know how to be alone and not defined by another person.
—**Oscar Wilde**

SECTION 5:
Encore Faith

As for me and my house, we will serve the Lord.
—Joshua 24:15

Chapter 19

Deepening (or Discovering) Your Faith

For this is what the Lord has commanded us: "I have made you a light for the Gentiles, that you may bring salvation to the ends of the earth."
—**Acts 13:47**

Making the transition into the Encore Season will likely bring more flexibility and freedom into our schedules. As we have explored in other chapters, there will be more time and opportunity to develop and deepen our relationships and explore our passions. This includes our spiritual lives and the relationship we have with Father God. I have found my faith journey leads me to the most personal of any relationships in my life; perhaps you have found that in your spiritual walk as well. As children grow up and move away, the solitude that becomes more regular provides the perfect opportunity to dedicate ourselves to the relationship we have with our Heavenly Father.

For some families, the Growing Up and Juggling Act seasons may have focused the family's spiritual life on activities for the children to engage in faith-based activities: Sunday School, Catechism, youth groups, and more. Perhaps there were public events to mark the beginning of what you hoped would be a lifelong faith journey for your child, such as a baptism or First Communion.

For other families, the busyness of the Juggling Act season created obstacles to regular participation in church or religious activities. Youth sports, dance competitions, and other commitments may have taken over every day of the week, including Sundays, during those chaotic years.

Whatever your spiritual journey may have been during those busy decades, the often quiet and less eventful reality of the Encore Season provides plenty of time for deepening your faith or perhaps discovering faith for the first time.

These opportunities may include:

- Visiting other churches or denominations.

- Joining a Bible study.

- Volunteering at a local MOPS (Mothers of Preschoolers) chapter.

- Attending a spiritual retreat or conference.

- Going on a mission trip.

- Going on a trip to the Holy Land.

- Dedicating regular time for prayer.

EXPLORING THE NEXT SEASON

In the Encore Season, we realize our time in this life is temporary. We come face-to-face with our physical mortality regularly as we walk the final steps of life's journey with those we know and love. We attend more funerals of our friends and, either quickly or slowly, come to the realization that one day, *we* will be the person others will be honoring and mourning.

How can we find peace and comfort as we walk through the final stage of our life's journey?

A Protestant confessional document called *The Heidelberg Catechism*[1] was published in 1953 in Heidelberg, Germany, and explores the Christian faith in a series of questions and answers. The document begins with that very question:

LORD'S DAY ONE[2]

Question: What is your only comfort in life and death?

Answer: That I am not my own, but belong with body and soul, both in life and in death, to my faithful Saviour Jesus Christ. He has fully paid for all my sins with his precious blood, and has set me free from all the power of the devil. He also preserves me in such a way that without the will of my heavenly Father not a hair can fall from my head; indeed, all things must work together for my salvation. Therefore, by his Holy Spirit he also assures me of eternal life and makes me heartily willing and ready from now on to live for him.

---

1. http://www.heidelberg-catechism.com/en/.

2. "Lord's Day 1." Heidelberg Catechism. Canadian Reformed Theological Seminary, Accessed May 23, 2023. http://www.heidelberg-catechism.com/en/lords-days/1.html.

Indeed, the Encore Season can provide time for reflecting on op-portunities and for discovering or strengthening a journey of faith. Opening your heart and soul to embrace the solitude and peaceful quiet in this season of life can provide you with hope as you forge relationships and look for the deeper meanings in life and the time that is still to come.

PLANNING YOUR ENCORE

- Think back to your Growing Up years. What activities did you engage in to discover or deepen your faith?

- How would you describe your spiritual life? How can you connect to a deeper spiritual life in your Encore Season?

- If you have never had a walk of faith, is there someone you can reach out to for a conversation?

For God so loved the world that he gave his one and only Son, that whoever believes in him shall not perish but have eternal life.
—John 3:16

Chapter 20

Christian Connections in the Encore Season

They devoted themselves to the apostles' teaching and to fellowship, to the breaking of bread and to prayer.
   —**Acts 2:42**

Attending a church service is only a part of the spiritual development that takes place in a body of faith. From the worship, prayer, and sermon that defines a traditional Sunday morning (and perhaps additional service Sunday evening), there are six other days of the week where a faith connection may not happen for older adults. During the Growing Up season, there are typically youth groups for middle school and high school students to attend. Even into the Young Adult season, many churches will encourage a time for deeper connection and fellowship. By the time the Encore Season rolls around, the options are often limited (at best). Why is that?

MOTHERS OF PRESCHOOLERS (MOPS)

At most churches, there is a local chapter of an international organization called MOPS. MOPS is an acronym for Mothers of Preschoolers. The organization started in the 1970s as a support group (of sorts) for young moms. In many churches, it is a vital epicenter for young women to come together to support and encourage each other through the often-tumultuous journey of mothering young children. The groups typically meet every week or every other week during the school year, even arranging on-site childcare so these moms can engage, connect, and socialize with their peers.

This organization has grown significantly through the years, with chapters now found in over sixty countries. People are people, and moms are moms, no matter their language or skin color.

Many of the weekly meetings include a Bible story and a spiritual development activity, in addition to refreshments. The fellowship is perhaps the most vital part of these gatherings, as these women share so much about life with one another, turning to each other for guidance, support, and advice. They share laughter and tears and vow to consistently pray for one another through any times of hardship, the trials in life, and through the joyful times too.

THE NEXT STAGE (MOMSnext)

Besides expanding geographically, MOPS has expanded through the years to include a MOMSnext subgroup designed for moms with older kids who want to continue these special connections and unique communities. This next group also provides the emotional and sometimes physical support many mothers need as children transition to adolescence and young adulthood. While there aren't as many of the MOMSnext groups, those that are active provide at least twice-monthly meetings, with more flexibility in schedule, activities, and curriculum.

WHAT ABOUT THE ENCORE SEASON? (GRANDPARENTS OF PRESCHOOLERS—GOPS)

I've often thought the MOPS organization should create an extension of its program and call it GOPS (Grandparents of Preschoolers). There is perhaps an even more significant lack of social connectedness and changes to make when our homes are no longer filled with the chaos and activity that comes with raising children. This group would be open to anyone adjusting to this new stage in life—the stage when the kids are leaving the nest and getting married and grandchildren come along. So, even though the blessing of being a grandparent of a preschooler may not have happened yet, anyone adjusting to this new life stage would be welcome in the organization.

There is a need for special connections and the development of a close relationship with a fellow believer during this challenging adjustment period. Our children are getting married and building their nests. A time when having a special group of fellow believers who are also going through or who have already gone through this same period of change can prove to be the most important and comfortable relationship we can build.

Since this type of organization does not exist (yet), perhaps you might consider pulling together your own group. Invite friends from work, church, or your neighborhood to meet regularly to discuss the issues everyone is facing, has faced already, or will face in the future. Get creative! Structure the meetings like a book club or discussion group—schedule outings and adventures. Encourage the rest of the group to invite people they know in the same life stage. You may find excellent new relationships evolve from a group of fellow believers who can learn to understand, trust, and lean on one another to find peace, joy, and hope in this new season of life.

PLANNING YOUR ENCORE

- Do you have a community of fellow Christians in your life? Make a list of people who are also in the Encore Season who share your faith.

- Consider coordinating opportunities where you can spend time together in a group for conversation, encouragement, and support.

- What are ways you can challenge and serve one another in ways that will help each other deepen your faith?

Therefore encourage one another and build each other up, just as in fact you are doing.
—1 Thessalonians 5:11

Chapter 21

Prayer in the Encore Season

And the peace of God, which transcends all understanding, will guard your hearts and your minds in Christ Jesus.
—**Philippians 4:7**

Transitioning into the Encore Season means the house is often silent. Where there used to be pandemonium, chaos, noise, music, laughing, dancing, yelling, and sometimes fighting, there is now often stillness. While maybe not literally, the quiet can seem deafening.

This quiet time also provides an excellent opportunity to reconnect with God—an opportunity for quiet times of prayer and reflection. Psalm 46:10 says, "Be still and know that I am God; I will be exalted among the nations, I will be exalted in the earth."

Our time to nurture our spiritual life is no longer only what we can cram between other activities and chores. We have the opportunity to sit down and read the Bible, write in a prayer journal, and spend time truly listening for God's voice in our lives.

LISTEN FOR GOD'S VOICE

When our schedules were full and our days were overwhelmingly busy, we would have to strain to hear God's voice in the storm. Now, we can hear God's whisper to us in the calm. When we feel there is no one to listen to us and no one to communicate with, we know there is always one essential relationship we have . . . with the One who has a dedicated listening ear when we need it the most.

We are never alone. When our homes may seem big and empty, God is there. Just as he was during the chaotic years, those years when we only cried out for help to get everything we needed to accomplish done. This time around, we need reassurance, to understand that the calm, quiet, and stillness are a part of God's journey for us as well.

God says in Jeremiah, "Call on me and come and pray to me, and I will listen to you" (29:12). Yet our prayer life and spiritual development were probably put on the back burner for so many years. We just could not find enough quiet time in the day. We were exhausted and weary. It is in this season when our schedule may seem so empty, our spiritual life may indeed become full. Perhaps fuller than ever before for many of us.

PLANNING YOUR ENCORE

- How will your prayer life be transformed with more "un-committed hours" each day?

- Consider what it means for you to pray. Does prayer seem like a solemn and intentional act of bowing your head or crossing your fingers? Or does prayer seem like a perpetual conversation going on in your head?

- What do you share with God? Does prayer focus on your wants and needs, or is it a time for thanksgiving? He wants to hear it all! Write an authentic, conversational prayer below. There is no wrong way to do it. Just be you.

Do not be anxious about anything, but in every situation, by prayer and petition, with thanksgiving, present your requests to God. And the peace of God, which transcends all understanding, will guard your hearts and your minds in Christ Jesus.
—Philippians 4:6–7

Conclusion

Twenty years from now you will be more disappointed by the things you didn't do than the by the ones that you did do.
—Mark Twain

It's easy to imagine an encore from the perspective of a member of the audience. If we think about it in a concert setting, we finish watching the performance and anxiously wait for the entertainers to come back onto the stage for their final song.

We watch.

We wait.

Then we cheer.

In this season of life, our challenge is to think of ourselves not as members of the audience but instead as performers. We are the individuals waiting behind the curtain—the ones getting ready to step onto the stage.

We get the chance to choose our next act. Will the next adventure be something new and fresh, or will we circle back to repeat some of our earlier hits?

Consider the Encore Season as a time for looking forward. After spending decades of your life putting everyone else first, you now get the chance to spend your time, talent, and treasure to take center stage in your own story.

Challenge yourself to make the rest of your life *the best of your life.*

About the Author

As a television meteorologist, Terri DeBoer delivered West Michigan's "wake up" weather for more than three decades. She has also served as co-host of a daily lifestyle show called *eight West*.

In 2021, Terri launched her first encore by becoming a published author. Terri's literary debut came with the release of *Brighter Skies Ahead: Forecasting a Full Life When You Empty The Nest.* Terri followed up the release of the book and companion journal by partnering with Faith Hospice to serve as primary author of *Grieving Well: A Healing Journey Through The Season of Grief,* released in February 2023. In Spring 2024, Terri will release a 366-day devotional for empty nesters.

Professionally, Terri is celebrating her own encore, retiring from a three-decades-long career as a broadcast meteorologist to launch a new career in the financial industry. In October, 2023, Terri joined the team at Jacobs Financial Services as Director of Communications. In her new role, Terri is excited to work with others who are approaching or entering their own "Encore Seasons". Terri is also expanding her literary focus; with more books of her own and helping others create books to share their own messaging and stories.

Personally, Terri is a married mother of three married adult children. She has also just welcomed her second grandchild. Terri resides in Byron Center, Michigan. Connect with Terri at:

www.terrideboer.com.

Made in the USA
Thornton, CO
11/24/23 06:00:22

ad2c3659-2fe4-4432-ab7a-9e0ef2032a82R01